Lord Lytton

Kenelm Chillingly His Adventures and Opinions

Lord Lytton

Kenelm Chillingly His Adventures and Opinions

ISBN/EAN: 9783742854513

Manufactured in Europe, USA, Canada, Australia, Japa

Cover: Foto ©Thomas Meinert / pixelio.de

Manufactured and distributed by brebook publishing software
(www.brebook.com)

Lord Lytton

Kenelm Chillingly His Adventures and Opinions

COLLECTION

OF

BRITISH AUTHORS

TAUCHNITZ EDITION.

VOL. 1308.

KENELM CHILLINGLY
BY EDWARD BULWER, LORD LYTTON.

IN FOUR VOLUMES.
VOL. I.

KENELM CHILLINGLY

HIS

ADVENTURES AND OPINIONS

BY

EDWARD BULWER, LORD LYTTON.

COPYRIGHT EDITION.

IN FOUR VOLUMES.

VOL. I.

LEIPZIG

BERNHARD TAUCHNITZ

1873.

KENELM CHILLINGLY.

BOOK I.

CHAPTER I.

SIR PETER CHILLINGLY, of Exmundham, Baronet, F.R.S. and F.A.S., was the representative of an ancient family, and a landed proprietor of some importance. He had married young, not from any ardent inclination for the connubial state, but in compliance with the request of his parents. They took the pains to select his bride; and if they might have chosen better they might have chosen worse, which is more than can be said for many men who choose wives for themselves. Miss Caroline Brotherton was in all respects a suitable connection. She had a pretty fortune, which was of much use in buying a couple of farms, long desiderated by the Chillinglys as necessary for the rounding of their

property into a ring-fence. She was highly con-
nected, and brought into the county that experience of fashionable life acquired by a young
lady who has attended a course of balls for three
seasons, and gone out in matrimonial honours,
with credit to herself and her chaperon. She
was handsome enough to satisfy a husband's
pride, but not so handsome as to keep perpetu-
ally on the *qui vive* a husband's jealousy. She
was considered highly accomplished; that is, she
played upon the pianoforte so that any musician
would say she "was very well taught;" but no
musician would go out of his way to hear her a
second time. She painted in water-colours—well
enough to amuse herself. She knew French and
Italian with an elegance so lady-like, that, without having read more than selected extracts from
authors in those languages, she spoke them both
with an accent more correct than we have any
reason to attribute to Rousseau or Ariosto. What
else a young lady may acquire in order to be
styled highly accomplished I do not pretend to
know, but I am sure that the young lady in ques-

tion fulfilled that requirement in the opinion of
the best masters. It was not only an eligible
match for Sir Peter Chillingly,—it was a brilliant
match. It was also a very unexceptionable match
for Miss Caroline Brotherton. This excellent
couple got on together as most excellent couples
do. A short time after marriage, Sir Peter, by
the death of his parents—who, having married
their heir, had nothing left in life worth the
trouble of living for—succeeded to the hereditary
estates; he lived for nine months of the year at
Exmundham, going to town for the other three
months. Lady Chillingly and himself were both
very glad to go to town, being bored at Exmundham; and very glad to go back to Exmundham,
being bored in town. With one exception it was
an exceedingly happy marriage, as marriages go.
Lady Chillingly had her way in small things; Sir
Peter his way in great. Small things happen
every day, great things once in three years. Once
in three years Lady Chillingly gave way to Sir
Peter; households so managed go on regularly.
The exception to their connubial happiness was,

after all, but of a negative description. Their affection was such that they sighed for a pledge of it; fourteen years had he and Lady Chillingly remained unvisited by the little stranger.

Now, in default of male issue, Sir Peter's estates passed to a distant cousin as heir-at-law; and during the last four years this heir-at-law had evinced his belief that, practically speaking, he was already heir-apparent; and (though Sir Peter was a much younger man than himself, and as healthy as any man well can be) had made his expectations of a speedy succession unpleasantly conspicuous. He had refused his consent to a small exchange of lands with a neighbouring squire, by which Sir Peter would have obtained some good arable land for an outlying unprofitable wood that produced nothing but fagots and rabbits, with the blunt declaration that he, the heir-at-law, was fond of rabbit-shooting, and that the wood would be convenient to him next season if he came into the property by that time, which he very possibly might. He disputed Sir Peter's right to make his customary fall of timber, and had even threatened him with a bill in Chancery on that subject. In short, this heir-at-law was exactly one of those persons to spite whom a landed proprietor would, if single, marry at the age of eighty in the hope of a family.

Nor was it only on account of his very natural wish to frustrate the expectations of this unamiable relation that Sir Peter Chillingly lamented the absence of the little stranger. Although belonging to that class of country gentlemen to whom certain political reasoners deny the intelligence vouchsafed to other members of the community, Sir Peter was not without a considerable degree of book-learning, and a great taste for speculative philosophy. He sighed for a legitimate inheritor to the stores of his erudition, and, being a very benevolent man, for a more active and useful dispenser of those benefits to the human race which philosophers confer by striking hard against each other; just as, how full soever of sparks a flint may be, they might lurk concealed in the flint till doomsday, if the flint were not hit by the steel. Sir Peter, in short, longed for a son amply endowed with the combative quality, in which he himself was deficient, but which is the first essential to all seekers after renown, and especially to benevolent philosophers.

Under these circumstances one may well conceive the joy that filled the household of Exmundham and extended to all the tenantry on that venerable estate, by whom the present possessor was much beloved, and the prospect of an heir-at-law with a special eye to the preservation of rabbits much detested, when the medical attendant of the Chillinglys declared that 'her ladyship was in an interesting way;' and to what height that joy culminated when, in due course of time, a male baby was safely enthroned in his cradle. To that cradle Sir Peter was summoned. He entered the room with a lively bound and a radiant countenance: he quitted it with a musing step and an overclouded brow.

Yet the baby was no monster. It did not come into the world with two heads, as some babies are said to have done; it was formed as babies are in general—was on the whole a thriving baby, a fine baby. Nevertheless, its aspect awed the father as already it had awed the nurse. The creature looked so unutterably solemn. It fixed its eyes upon Sir Peter with a melancholy reproachful stare; its lips were compressed and drawn downward as if discontentedly meditating its future destinies. The nurse declared in a frightened whisper that it had uttered no cry on facing the light. It had taken possession of its cradle in all the dignity of silent sorrow. A more saddened and a more thoughtful countenance a human being could not exhibit if he were leaving the world instead of entering it.

"Hem!" said Sir Peter to himself on regaining the solitude of his library; "a philosopher who contributes a new inhabitant to this vale of tears takes upon himself very anxious responsibilities——"

At that moment the joy-bells rang out from the neighbouring church-tower, the summer sun shone into the windows, the bees hummed among the flowers on the lawn: Sir Peter roused himself and looked forth—"After all," said he, cheerily, "the vale of tears is not without a smile."

CHAPTER II.

A FAMILY council was held at Exmundham
Hall to deliberate on the name by which this
remarkable infant should be admitted into the
Christian community. The junior branches of
that ancient house consisted, first, of the ob-
noxious heir-at-law — a Scotch branch — named
Chillingly Gordon. He was the widowed father
of one son, now of the age of three, and happily
unconscious of the injury inflicted on his future
prospects by the advent of the new-born; which
could not be truthfully said of his Caledonian
father. Mr. Chillingly Gordon was one of those
men who get on in the world without our being
able to discover why. His parents died in his
infancy, and left him nothing; but the family interest procured him an admission into the Charter
House School, at which illustrious academy he
obtained no remarkable distinction. Nevertheless

as soon as he left it the State took him under its special care, and appointed him to a clerkship in a public office. From that moment he continued to get on in the world, and was now a commissioner of customs, with a salary of £1500 a-year. As soon as he had been thus enabled to maintain a wife, he selected a wife who assisted to maintain himself. She was an Irish peer's widow, with a jointure of £2000 a-year.

A few months after his marriage, Chillingly Gordon effected insurances on his wife's life, so as to secure himself an annuity of £1000 a-year in case of her decease. As she appeared to be a fine healthy woman, some years younger than her husband, the deduction from his income effected by the annual payments for the insurance seemed an over-sacrifice of present enjoyment to future contingencies. The result bore witness to his reputation for sagacity, as the lady died in the second year of their wedding, a few months after the birth of her only child, and of a heart-disease which had been latent to the doctors, but which, no doubt, Gordon had affectionately discovered before he had insured a life too valuable not to need some compensation for its loss. He was now, then, in the possession of £2500 a-year, and was therefore very well off, in the pecuniary sense of the phrase. He had, moreover, acquired a reputation which gave him a social rank beyond that accorded to him by a discerning State. He was considered a man of solid judgment, and his opinion upon all matters, private and public, carried weight. The opinion itself, critically examined, was not worth much, but the way he announced it was imposing. Mr. Fox said that 'No one ever was so wise as Lord Thurlow looked.' Lord Thurlow could not have looked wiser than Mr. Chillingly Gordon. He had a square jaw and large red bushy eyebrows, which he lowered down with great effect when he delivered judgment. He had another advantage for acquiring grave reputation. He was a very unpleasant man. He could be rude if you contradicted him; and as few persons wish to provoke rudeness, so he was seldom contradicted.

Mr. Chillingly Mivers, another cadet of the house, was also distinguished, but in a different way. He was a bachelor, now about the age of thirty-five. He was eminent for a supreme well-bred contempt for everybody and everything. He was the originator and chief proprietor of a public journal called 'The Londoner,' which had lately been set up on that principle of contempt, and, we need not say, was exceedingly popular with those leading members of the community who admire nobody and believe in nothing. Mr. Chillingly Mivers was regarded by himself and by others as a man who might have achieved the highest success in any branch of literature, if he had deigned to exhibit his talents therein. But he did not so deign, and therefore he had full right to imply that, if he had written an epic, a drama, a novel, a history, a metaphysical treatise, Milton, Shakespeare, Cervantes, Hume, Berkeley would have been nowhere. He held greatly to the dignity of the anonymous; and even in the journal which he originated, nobody could ever ascertain what he wrote. But, at all events, Mr. Chillingly Mivers was what Mr. Chillingly Gordon was not—viz., a very clever man, and by no means an unpleasant one in general society.

The Rev. John Stalworth Chillingly was a decided adherent to the creed of what is called 'muscular Christianity,' and a very fine specimen of it too. A tall stout man with broad shoulders, and that division of lower limb which intervenes between the knee and the ankle powerfully developed. He would have knocked down a deist as soon as looked at him. It is told by the Sieur de Joinville, in his Memoir of Louis, the sainted king, that an assembly of divines and theologians convened the Jews of an oriental city for the purpose of arguing with them on the truths of Christianity, and a certain knight, who was at that time crippled, and supporting himself on crutches, asked and obtained permission to be present at the debate. The Jews flocked to the summons, when a prelate, selecting a learned rabbi, mildly put to him the leading question whether he owned the divine conception of our

Lord. "Certainly not," replied the rabbi; whereon the pious knight, shocked by such blasphemy, uplifted his crutch and felled the rabbi, and then flung himself among the other misbelievers, whom he soon dispersed in ignominious flight and in a very belaboured condition. The conduct of the knight was reported to the sainted king, with a request that it should be properly reprimanded; but the sainted king delivered himself of this wise judgment:—

"If a pious knight is a very learned clerk, and can meet in fair argument the doctrines of the misbeliever, by all means let him argue fairly; but if a pious knight is not a learned clerk, and the argument goes against him, then let the pious knight cut the discussion short by the edge of his good sword."

The Rev. John Stalworth Chillingly was of the same opinion as St. Louis; otherwise, he was a mild and amiable man. He encouraged cricket and other manly sports among his rural parishioners. He was a skilful and bold rider, but he did not hunt; a convivial man—and took his

bottle freely.   But his tastes in literature were of
a refined and peaceful character, contrasting therein
the tendencies one might have expected from his
muscular development of Christianity.   He was a
great reader of poetry, but he disliked Scott and
Byron, whom he considered flashy and noisy: he
maintained that Pope was only a versifier, and
that the greatest poet in the language was Wordsworth; he did not care much for the ancient clas-
sics; he refused all merit to the French poets; he
knew nothing of the Italian, but he dabbled in
German, and was inclined to bore one about the
Hermann and Dorothea of Goethe. He was married
to a homely little wife, who revered him in silence,
and thought there would be no schism in the
Church if he were in his right place as Archbishop of Canterbury: in this opinion he entirely
agreed with his wife.

Besides these three male specimens of the
Chillingly race, the fairer sex was represented, in
the absence of her ladyship, who still kept her
room, by three female Chillinglys—sisters of Sir
Peter—and all three spinsters. Perhaps one reason

why they had remained single was, that externally
they were so like each other that a suitor must
have been puzzled which to choose, and may
have been afraid that if he did choose one, he
should be caught next day kissing another one in
mistake. They were all tall, all thin, with long
throats—and beneath the throats a fine development of bone. They had all pale hair, pale eye-
lids, pale eyes, and pale complexions. They all
dressed exactly alike, and their favourite colour
was a vivid green: they were so dressed on this
occasion.

As there was such similitude in their persons,
so, to an ordinary observer, they were exactly
the same in character and mind. Very well behaved, with proper notions of female decorum—
very distant and reserved in manner to strangers
—very affectionate to each other and their relations or favourites—very good to the poor, whom
they looked upon as a different order of creation,
and treated with that sort of benevolence which
humane people bestow upon dumb animals. Their
minds had been nourished on the same books—

what one read the others had read. The books were mainly divided into two classes—novels, and what they called "good books." They had a habit of taking a specimen of each alternately —one day a novel, then a good book, then a novel again, and so on. Thus if the imagination was overwarmed on Monday, on Tuesday it was cooled down to a proper temperature; and if frost-bitten on Tuesday, it took a tepid bath on Wednesday. The novels they chose were indeed rarely of a nature to raise the intellectual thermometer into blood-heat: the heroes and heroines were models of correct conduct. Mr. James's novels were then in vogue, and they united in saying that those "*were* novels a father might allow his daughters to read." But though an ordinary observer might have failed to recognise any distinction between these three ladies, and, finding them habitually dressed in green, would have said they were as much alike as one pea is to another, they had their idiosyncratic differences, when duly examined. Miss Margaret, the eldest, was the commanding one of the three; it was she

who regulated their household (they all lived together), kept the joint purse, and decided every
doubtful point that arose,—whether they should
or should not ask Mrs. So-and-so to tea—whether
Mary should or should not be discharged—whether or not they should go to Broadstairs or to
Sandgate for the month of October. In fact, Miss
Margaret was the WILL of the body corporate.

Miss Sibyl was of milder nature and more
melancholic temperament; she had a poetic turn
of mind, and occasionally wrote verses. Some
of these had been printed on satin paper, and
sold for objects of beneficence at charity bazaars.
The county newspapers said that the verses "were
characterised by all the elegance of a cultured
and feminine mind." The other two sisters agreed
that Sibyl was the genius of the household, but,
like all geniuses, not sufficiently practical for the
world. Miss Sarah Chillingly, the youngest of the
three, and now just in her forty-fourth year, was
looked upon by the others as 'a dear thing, inclined to be naughty, but such a darling that nobody could have the heart to scold her.' Miss

Margaret said 'she was a giddy creature.' Miss
Sibyl wrote a poem on her, entitled—

"Warning to a young Lady against the Pleasures of the World."

They called her Sally; the other two sisters
had no diminutive synonyms. Sally is a name
indicative of fastness. But this Sally would not
have been thought fast in another household,
and she was now little likely to sally out of the
one she belonged to. These sisters, who were
all many years older than Sir Peter, lived in a
handsome old-fashioned red-brick house, with a
large garden at the back, in the principal street
of the capital of their native county. They had
each £10,000 for portion; and if he could have
married all three, the heir-at-law would have married them, and settled the aggregate £30,000 on
himself. But we have not yet come to recognise
Mormonism as legal, though, if our social progress
continues to slide in the same grooves as at
present, heaven only knows what triumphs over
the prejudices of our ancestors may not be
achieved by the wisdom of our descendants!

CHAPTER III.

SIR PETER stood on his hearthstone, surveyed the guests seated in semicircle, and said: "Friends, —in Parliament, before anything affecting the fate of a Bill is discussed, it is, I believe, necessary to introduce the Bill." He paused a moment, rang the bell, and said to the servant who entered, "Tell nurse to bring in the Baby."

MR. GORDON CHILLINGLY.—"I don't see the necessity for that, Sir Peter. We may take the existence of the Baby for granted."

MR. MIVERS.—"It is an advantage to the reputation of Sir Peter's work to preserve the incognito. *Omne ignotum pro magnifico.*"

THE REV. JOHN STALWORTH CHILLINGLY.—"I don't approve the cynical levity of such remarks. Of course we must all be anxious to see, in the earliest stage of being, the future representative of our name and race. Who would not wish to contemplate the source, however small, of the Tigris or the Nile!——"

Miss Sally (tittering).—"He! he!"   .

Miss Margaret. — "For shame, you giddy thing!"

The Baby enters in the nurse's arms. All rise and gather round the Baby, with one exception—Mr. Gordon, who has ceased to be heir-at-law.

The Baby returned the gaze of its relations with the most contemptuous indifference. Miss Sibyl was the first to pronounce an opinion on the Baby's attributes. Said she, in a solemn whisper—"What a heavenly mournful expression! it seems so grieved to have left the angels!"

· The Rev. John.—"That is prettily said, cousin Sibyl; but the infant must pluck up its courage and fight its way among mortals with a good heart, if it wants to get back to the angels again. And I think it will; a fine child." He took it from the nurse, and moving it deliberately up and down, as if to weigh it, said cheerfully, "Monstrous heavy! by the time it is twenty it will be a match for a prize-fighter of fifteen stone!"

Therewith he stróde to Gordon, who, as if to show that he now considered himself wholly apart from all interest in the affairs of a family that had so ill-treated him in the birth of that Baby, had taken up the 'Times' newspaper and concealed his countenance beneath the ample sheet. The Parson abruptly snatched away the 'Times' with one hand, and, with the other substituting to the indignant eyes of the *ci-devant* heir-at-law the spectacle of the Baby, said, "Kiss it."

"Kiss it!" echoed Chillingly Gordon, pushing back his chair—"kiss it! pooh, sir, stand off! I never kissed my own baby; I shall not kiss another man's. Take the thing away, sir; it is ugly; it has black eyes."

Sir Peter, who was near-sighted, put on his spectacles and examined the face of the newborn. "True," said he, "it has black eyes—very extraordinary — portentous; the first Chillingly that ever had black eyes."

"Its mamma has black eyes," said Miss Margaret; "it takes after its mamma; it has not the fair beauty of the Chillinglys, but it is not ugly."

"Sweet infant!" sighed Sibyl; "and so good —does not cry."

"It has neither cried nor crowed since it was born," said the nurse; "bless its little heart!"

She took the Baby from the Parson's arms, and smoothed back the frill of its cap, which had got ruffled.

"You may go now, nurse," said Sir Peter.

CHAPTER IV.

"I AGREE with Mr. Shandy," said Sir Peter, resuming his stand on the hearthstone, "that among the responsibilities of a parent the choice of a name which his child is to bear for life is one of the gravest. And this is especially so with those who belong to the order of baronets. In the case of a peer, his Christian name, fused in his titular designation, disappears. In the case of a Mister, if his baptismal be cacophonous or provocative of ridicule, he need not ostentatiously parade it; he may drop it altogether on his visiting cards, and may be imprinted as Mr. Jones instead of Mr. Ebenezer Jones. In his signature, save where the forms of the law demand Ebenezer in full, he may only use an initial, and be your obedient servant E. Jones, leaving it to be conjectured that E. stands for Edward or Ernest—names inoffensive, and not suggestive of a Dissenting Chapel, like Ebenezer. If a man called Edward or Ernest be detected in some youthful indiscretion, there is no indelible stain on his moral character; but if an Ebenezer be so detected, he is set down as a hypocrite—it produces that shock on the public mind which is felt when a professed saint is proved to be a bit of a sinner. But a baronet never can escape from his baptismal—it cannot lie *perdu*, it cannot shrink into an initial, it stands forth glaringly in the light of day; christen him Ebenezer, and he is Sir Ebenezer in full, with all its perilous consequences if he ever succumb to those temptations to which even baronets are exposed. But, my friends, it is not only the effect that the sound of a name has upon others which is to be thoughtfully considered; the effect that his name produces on the man himself is perhaps still more important. Some names stimulate and encourage the owner, others deject and paralyse him; I am a melancholy instance of that truth. Peter has been for many generations, as you are aware, the baptismal to which the eldest-born of our family has been devoted. On the altar of that name I have been sacrificed. Never has there been a Sir Peter Chillingly who has, in any way, distinguished himself above his fellows. That name has been a dead weight on my intellectual energies. In the catalogue of illustrious Englishmen there is, I think, no immortal Sir Peter, except Sir Peter Teazle, and he only exists on the comic stage."

MISS SIBYL. —"Sir Peter Lely?"

SIR PETER CHILLINGLY.—"That painter was not an Englishman. He was born in Westphalia, famous for hams. I confine my remarks to the children of our native land. I am aware that in foreign countries the name is not an extinguisher to the genius of its owner. But why? In other countries its sound is modified. Pierre Corneille was a great man; but I put it to you whether, had he been an Englishman, he could have been the father of European tragedy as Peter Crow?"

MISS SIBYL.—"Impossible!"

MISS SALLY.—"He! he!"

MISS MARGARET.—"There is nothing to laugh at, you giddy child!"

SIR PETER.—"My son shall not be petrified into Peter."

MR. GORDON CHILLINGLY.—"If a man is such a fool—and I don't say your son will not be a fool, cousin Peter—as to be influenced by the sound of his own name, and you want the booby to turn the world topsy-turvy, you had better call him Julius Cæsar, or Hannibal, or Attila, or Charlemagne."

SIR PETER (who excels mankind in imperturbability of temper).—"On the contrary, if you inflict upon a man the burthen of one of those names, the glory of which he cannot reasonably expect to eclipse or even to equal, you crush him beneath the weight. If a poet were called John Milton or William Shakespeare, he could not dare to publish even a sonnet. No; the choice of a name lies between the two extremes of ludicrous insignificance and oppressive renown. For this reason I have ordered the family pedigree to be suspended on yonder wall. Let us examine

it with care, and see whether, among the Chillinglys themselves or their alliances, we can discover
a name that can be borne with becoming dignity
by the destined head of our house—a name
neither too light nor too heavy."

Sir Peter here led the way to the family tree—
a goodly roll of parchment, with the arms of the
family emblazoned at the top. Those arms were
simple, as ancient heraldic coats are—three fishes
argent on a field *azur;* the crest a mermaid's
head. All flocked to inspect the pedigree except
Mr. Gordon, who resumed the 'Times' newspaper.

"I never could quite make out what kind of
fishes these are," said the Rev. John Stalworth.
"They are certainly not pike, which formed the
emblematic blazon of the Hotofts, and are still
grim enough to frighten future Shakespeares, on
the scutcheon of the Warwickshire Lucys."

"I believe they are tenches," said Mr. Mivers.
"The tench is a fish that knows how to keep itself safe, by a philosophical taste for an obscure
existence in deep holes and slush."

SIR PETER.—"No, Mivers; the fishes are dace,
a fish that, once introduced into any pond, never
can be got out again. You may drag the water—
you may let off the water—you may say 'Those
dace are extirpated,'—vain thought!—the dace
reappear as before; and in this respect the arms
are really emblematic of the family. All the dis-
orders and revolutions that have occurred in England since the Heptarchy have left the Chillinglys
the same race in the same place. Somehow or
other the Norman Conquest did not despoil them;
they held fiefs under Eudo Dapifer as peacefully
as they had held them under King Harold; they
took no part in the Crusades, nor the Wars of
the Roses, nor the Civil Wars between Charles
the First and the Parliament. As the dace sticks
to the water, and the water sticks by the dace,
so the Chillinglys stuck to the land and the land
stuck by the Chillinglys. Perhaps I am wrong to
wish that the new Chillingly may be a little less
like a dace."

"Oh!" cried Miss Margaret, who, mounted
on a chair, had been inspecting the pedigree

through an eyeglass, "I don't see a fine Christian name from the beginning, except Oliver."

SIR PETER.—"That Chillingly was born in Oliver Cromwell's Protectorate, and named Oliver in compliment to him, as his father, born in the reign of James I., was christened James. The three fishes always swam with the stream. Oliver! —Oliver not a bad name, but significant of radical doctrines."

MR. MIVERS.—"I don't think so. Oliver Cromwell made short work of radicals and their doctrines; but perhaps we can find a name less awful and revolutionary."

"I have it—I have it," cried the Parson. "Here is a descent from Sir Kenelm Digby and Venetia Stanley. Sir Kenelm Digby! No finer specimen of muscular Christianity. He fought as well as he wrote;—eccentric, it is true, but always a gentleman. Call the boy Kenelm!"

"A sweet name," said Miss Sibyl—"it breathes of romance."

"Sir Kenelm Chillingly! It sounds well—imposing!" said Miss Margaret.

"And," remarked Mr. Mivers, "it has this advantage—that while it has sufficient association with honourable distinction to affect the mind of the namesake and rouse his emulation, it is not that of so stupendous a personage as to defy rivalry. Sir Kenelm Digby was certainly an accomplished and gallant gentleman; but what with his silly superstition about sympathetic powders, &c., any man nowadays might be clever in comparison without being a prodigy. Yes, let us decide on Kenelm."

Sir Peter meditated. "Certainly," said he, after a pause—"certainly the name of Kenelm carries with it very crotchety associations; and I am afraid that Sir Kenelm Digby did not make a prudent choice in marriage. The fair Venetia was no better than she should be; and I should wish my heir not to be led away by beauty, but wed a woman of respectable character and decorous conduct."

MISS MARGARET.—"A British matron, of course."

THREE SISTERS (in chorus).—"Of course—of course!"

"But," resumed Sir Peter, "I am crotchety myself, and crotchets are innocent things enough; and as for marriage, the Baby cannot marry to-morrow, so that we have ample time to consider that matter. Kenelm Digby was a man any family might be proud of; and, as you say, sister Margaret, Kenelm Chillingly does not sound amiss—Kenelm Chillingly it shall be!"

The Baby was accordingly christened Kenelm, after which ceremony its face grew longer than before.

CHAPTER V.

BEFORE his relations dispersed, Sir Peter summoned Mr. Gordon into his library.

"Cousin," said he, kindly, "I do not blame you for the want of family affection, or even of humane interest, which you exhibit towards the New-born."

"Blame me, cousin Peter! I should think not. I exhibit as much family affection and humane interest as could be expected from me—circumstances considered."

"I own," said Sir Peter, with all his wonted mildness, "that after remaining childless for fourteen years of wedded life, the advent of this little stranger must have occasioned you a disagreeable surprise. But, after all, as I am many years younger than you, and, in the course of nature, shall outlive you, the loss is less to yourself than to your son, and upon that I wish to say a few words. You know too well the conditions on which I hold my estate not to be aware that I have not legally the power to saddle it with any bequest to your boy. The New-born succeeds to the fee-simple as last in tail. But I intend, from this moment, to lay by something every year for your son out of my income; and, fond as I am of London for a part of the year, I shall now give up my town-house. If I live to the years the Psalmist allots to man, I shall thus accumulate something handsome for your son, which may be taken in the way of compensation."

Mr. Gordon was by no means softened by this generous speech. However, he answered more politely than was his wont, "My son will be very much obliged to you, should he ever need your intended bequest." Pausing a moment, he added, with a cheerful smile, "A large percentage of infants die before attaining the age of twenty-one."

"Nay, but I am told your son is an uncommonly fine healthy child."

"My son, cousin Peter! I was not thinking of

my son, but of yours. Yours has a big head.
I should not wonder if he had water in it. I
don't wish to alarm you, but he may go off any
day, and in that case it is not likely that Lady
Chillingly will condescend to replace him. So
you will excuse me if I still keep a watchful eye
on my rights; and however painful to my feelings,
I must still dispute your right to cut a stick of
the field timber."

"That is nonsense, Gordon. I am tenant for
life without impeachment of waste, and can cut
down all timber not ornamental."

"I advise you not, cousin Peter. I have told
you before that I shall try the question at
law, should you provoke it,—amicably, of course.
Rights are rights; and if I am driven to maintain
mine, I trust that you are of a mind too liberal
to allow your family affection to me and mine to
be influenced by a decree of the Court of Chancery. But my fly is waiting. I must not miss
the train."

"Well, good-bye, Gordon. Shake hands."

"Shake hands!—of course—of course. By the

by, as I came through the lodge, it seemed to me sadly out of repair. I believe you are liable for dilapidations. Good-bye."

"The man is a hog in armour," soliloquised Sir Peter, when his cousin was gone; "and if it be hard to drive a common pig in the way he don't choose to go, a hog in armour is indeed undrivable. But his boy ought not to suffer for his father's hoggishness; and I shall begin at once to see what I can lay by for him. After all, it *is* hard upon Gordon. Poor Gordon!—poor fellow—poor fellow! Still I hope he will not go to law with me. I hate law. And a worm will turn—especially a worm that is put into Chancery."

CHAPTER VI.

DESPITE the sinister semi-predictions of the *ci-devant* heir-at-law, the youthful Chillingly passed with safety, and indeed with dignity, through the infant stages of existence. He took his measles and whooping-cough with philosophical equanimity. He gradually acquired the use of speech, but he did not too lavishly exercise that special attribute of humanity. During the earlier years of child-hood he spoke as little as if he had been prematurely trained in the school of Pythagoras. But he evidently spoke the less in order to reflect the more. He observed closely and pondered deeply over what he observed. At the age of eight he began to converse more freely, and it was in that year that he startled his mother with the question —"Mamma, are you not sometimes overpowered by the sense of your own identity?"

Lady Chillingly—I was about to say rushed,

but Lady Chillingly never rushed—Lady Chillingly glided less sedately than her wont to Sir Peter and, repeating her son's question, said, "The boy is growing troublesome, too wise for any woman; he must go to school."

Sir Peter was of the same opinion. But where on earth did the child get hold of so long a word as "identity," and how did so extraordinary and puzzling a metaphysical question come into his head? Sir Peter summoned Kenelm, and ascertained that the boy, having free access to the library, had fastened upon Locke on the Human Understanding, and was prepared to dispute with that philosopher upon the doctrine of innate ideas. Quoth Kenelm, gravely—"A want is an idea; and if, as soon as I was born, I felt the want of food and knew at once where to turn for it, without being taught, surely I came into the world with an 'innate idea.'"

Sir Peter, though he dabbled in metaphysics, was posed, and scratched his head without getting out a proper answer as to the distinction between ideas and instincts. "My child," he said at last, "you don't know what you are talking about; go and take a good gallop on your black pony; and I forbid you to read any books that are not given to you by myself or your mamma. Stick to Puss in Boots."

CHAPTER VII.

SIR PETER ordered his carriage and drove to the house of the stout Parson. That doughty ecclesiastic held a family living a few miles distant from the Hall, and was the only one of the cousins with whom Sir Peter habitually communed on his domestic affairs.

He found the Parson in his study, which exhibited tastes other than clerical. Over the chimney-piece were ranged fencing-foils, boxing-gloves, and staffs for the athletic exercise of single-stick; cricket-bats and fishing-rods filled up the angles. There were sundry prints on the walls; one of Mr. Wordsworth, flanked by two of distinguished race-horses; one of a Leicestershire short-horn, with which the Parson, who farmed his own glebe and bred cattle in its rich pastures, had won a prize at the county show; and on either side of that animal were the portraits of

Hooker and Jeremy Taylor. There were dwarf bookcases containing miscellaneous works very handsomely bound. At the open window, a stand of flower-pots, the flowers in full bloom. The Parson's flowers were famous.

The appearance of the whole room was that of a man who is tidy and neat in his habits.

"Cousin," said Sir Peter, "I have come to consult you." And therewith he related the marvellous precocity of Kenelm Chillingly. "You see the name begins to work on him rather too much. He must go to school; and now what school shall it be? Private or public?"

THE REV. JOHN STALWORTH.—"There is a great deal to be said for or against either. At a public school the chances are that Kenelm will no longer be overpowered by a sense of his own identity; he will more probably lose identity altogether. The worst of a public school is that a sort of common character is substituted for individual character. The master, of course, can't attend to the separate development of each boy's idiosyncrasy. All minds are thrown into one' great mould, and come out of it more or less in the same form. An Etonian may be clever or stupid, but, as either, he remains emphatically Etonian. A public school ripens talent, but its tendency is to stifle genius. Then, too, a public school for an only son, heir to a good estate, which will be entirely at his own disposal, is apt to encourage reckless and extravagant habits; and your estate requires careful management, and leaves no margin for an heir's notes-of-hand and post-obits. On the whole, I am against a public school for Kenelm."

"Well, then, we will decide on a private one."

"Hold!" said the Parson: "a private school has its drawbacks. You can seldom produce large fishes in small ponds. In private schools the competition is narrowed, the energies stinted. The schoolmaster's wife interferes, and generally coddles the boys. There is not manliness enough in those academies; no fagging, and very little fighting. A clever boy turns out a prig; a boy of feebler intellect turns out a well-behaved young lady in trousers. Nothing muscular in the system.

Decidedly * the namesake and descendant* of
Kenelm Digby should not go to a private semi-
nary."

"So far as I gather from your reasoning,"
said Sir Peter, with characteristic placidity,
"Kenelm Chillingly is not to go to school at all."

"It does look like it," said the Parson, candidly; "but, on consideration, there is a medium.
There are schools which unite the best qualities
of public and private schools, large enough to
stimulate and develop energies mental and physical, yet not so framed as to melt all character in
one crucible. For instance, there is a school
which has at this moment one of the first scholars
in Europe for head-master—a school which has
turned out some of the most remarkable men of
the rising generation. The master sees at a glance
if a boy be clever, and takes pains with him accordingly. He is not a mere teacher of hexame-
ters and sapphics. His learning embraces all
literature, ancient and modern. He is a good
writer and a fine critic—admires Wordsworth.
He winks at fighting, his boys know how to use

their fists, and they are not in the habit of sign-
ing post-obits before they are fifteen. Merton
School is the place for Kenelm."

"Thank you," said Sir Peter. "It is a great
comfort in life to find somebody who can decide
for one. I am an irresolute man myself, and in
ordinary matters willingly let Lady Chillingly
govern me."

"I should like to see a wife govern *me*," said
the stout Parson.

"But you are not married to Lady Chillingly.
And now let us go into the garden and look at
your dahlias."

———

CHAPTER VIII.

THE youthful confuter of Locke was despatched to Merton School, and ranked, according to his merits, as lag of the penultimate form. When he came home for the Christmas holidays he was more saturnine than ever—in fact, his countenance bore the impression of some absorbing grief. He said, however, that he liked school very well, and eluded all other questions. But early the next morning he mounted his black pony and rode to the Parson's rectory. The reverend gentleman was in his farmyard examining his bullocks when Kenelm accosted him thus briefly:—

"Sir, I am disgraced, and I shall die of it if you cannot help to set me right in my own eyes."

"My dear boy, don't talk in that way. Come into my study."

As soon as they entered that room, and the

Parson had carefully closed the door, he took the boy's arm, turned him round to the light, and saw at once that there was something very grave on his mind. Chucking him under the chin, the Parson said cheerily, "Hold up your head, Kenelm. I am sure you have done nothing unworthy of a gentleman."

"I don't know that. I fought a boy very little bigger than myself, and I have been licked. I did not give in, though; but the other boys picked me up, for I could not stand any longer—and the fellow is a great bully—and his name is Butt—and he's the son of a lawyer—and he got my head into chancery—and I have challenged him to fight again next half—and unless you can help me to lick him, I shall never be good for anything in the world—never. It will break my heart."

"I am very glad to hear you have had the pluck to challenge him. Just let me see how you double your fist. Well, that's not amiss. Now, put yourself into a fighting attitude, and hit out at me—hard—harder! Pooh! that will never do.

You should make your blows as straight as an
arrow. And that's not the way to stand. Stop—
so; well on your haunches—weight on the left
leg—good! Now, put on these gloves, and I'll
give you a lesson in boxing."

Five minutes afterwards Mrs. John Chillingly,
entering the room to summon her husband to
breakfast, stood astounded to see him with his
coat off, and parrying the blows of Kenelm, who
flew at him like a young tiger. The good pastor
at that moment might certainly have appeared a
fine type of muscular Christianity, but not of that
kind of Christianity out of which one makes Arch-
bishops of Canterbury.

"Good gracious me!" faltered Mrs. John Chillingly; and then, wife-like, flying to the protection
of her husband, she seized Kenelm by the shoulders, and gave him a good shaking. The Parson,
who was sadly out of breath, was not displeased
at the interruption, but took that opportunity to
put on his coat, and said, "We'll begin again to-
morrow. Now, come to breakfast." But during

breakfast Kenelm's face still betrayed dejection, and he talked little, and ate less.

As soon as the meal was over, he drew the Parson into the garden and said, "I have been thinking, sir, that perhaps it is not fair to Butt, that I should be taking these lessons; and if it is not fair, I'd rather not——"

"Give me your hand, my boy!" cried the Parson, transported. "The name of Kenelm is not thrown away upon you. The natural desire of man in his attribute of fighting animal (an attribute in which, I believe, he excels all other animated beings, except a quail and a gamecock), is to beat his adversary. But the natural desire of that culmination of man which we call gentleman, is to beat his adversary fairly. A gentleman would rather be beaten fairly than beat unfairly. Is not that your thought?"

"Yes," replied Kenelm, firmly; and then, beginning to philosophise, he added,—"And it stands to reason; because if I beat a fellow unfairly, I don't really beat him at all."

"Excellent! But suppose that you and an-

4*

other boy go into examination upon Cæsar's Com-
mentaries or the multiplication-table, and the other
boy is cleverer than you, but you have taken the
trouble to learn the subject and he has not; should
you say you beat him unfairly?"

Kenelm meditated a moment, and then said
decidedly, "No."

"That which applies to the use of your brains
applies equally to the use of your fists. Do you
comprehend me?"

"Yes, sir; I do now."

"In the time of your namesake, Sir Kenelm
Digby, gentlemen wore swords, and they learned
how to use them, because, in case of quarrel, they
had to fight with them. Nobody, at least in England, fights with swords now. It is a democratic
age, and if you fight at all, you are reduced to
fists; and if Kenelm Digby learned to fence, so
Kenelm Chillingly must learn to box; and if a
gentleman thrashes a drayman twice his size, who
has not learned to box, it is not unfair, it is but
an exemplification of the truth, that knowledge is

power. Come and take another lesson on boxing to-morrow."

Kenelm remounted his pony and returned home. He found his father sauntering in the garden with a book in his hand. "Papa," said Kenelm, "how does one gentleman write to another with whom he has a quarrel, and he don't want to make it up, but he has something to say about the quarrel which it is fair the other gentleman should know?"

"I don't understand what you mean."

"Well, just before I went to school I remember hearing you say that you had a quarrel with Lord Hautfort, and that he was an ass, and you would write and tell him so. When you wrote did you say, 'You are an ass'? Is that the way one gentleman writes to another?"

"Upon my honour, Kenelm, you ask very odd questions. But you cannot learn too early this fact, that irony is to the high-bred what billingsgate is to the vulgar; and when one gentleman thinks another gentleman an ass, he does not say it point-blank—he implies it in the politest terms he can invent. Lord Hautfort denies my right of free warren over a trout-stream that runs through his lands. I don't care a rush about the trout-stream, but there is no doubt of my right to fish in it. He was an ass to raise the question; for, if he had not, I should not have exercised the right. As he did raise the question, I was obliged to catch his trout."

"And you wrote a letter to him?"

"Yes."

"How did you write, papa? What did you say?"

"Something like this. 'Sir Peter Chillingly presents his compliments to Lord Hautfort, and thinks it fair to his lordship to say that he has taken the best legal advice with regard to his rights of free warren, and trusts to be forgiven if he presumes to suggest that Lord Hautfort might do well to consult his own lawyer before he decides on disputing them.'"

"Thank you, papa, I see——"

That evening Kenelm wrote the following letter:—

"Mr. Chillingly presents his compliments to Mr. Butt, and thinks it fair to Mr. Butt to say, that he is taking lessons in boxing, and trusts to be forgiven if he presumes to suggest that Mr. Butt might do well to take lessons himself before fighting with Mr. Chillingly next half."

"Papa," said Kenelm the next morning, "I want to write to a schoolfellow whose name is Butt; he is the son of a lawyer who is called a serjeant. I don't know where to direct to him."

"That is easily ascertained," said Sir Peter. "Serjeant Butt is an eminent man, and his address will be in the Court Guide." The address was found—Bloomsbury Square, and Kenelm directed his letter accordingly. In due course he received this answer:—

"You are an insolent little fool, and I'll thrash you within an inch of your life.

"ROBERT BUTT."

After the receipt of that polite epistle, Kenelm

Chillingly's scruples vanished, and he took daily
lessons in muscular Christianity.

Kenelm returned to school with a brow cleared
from care, and three days after his return he wrote
to the Rev. John:—

"DEAR SIR,—I have licked Butt.   Knowledge
is power.—Your affectionate

"KENELM.

"*P.S.*—Now that I have licked Butt, I have
made it up with him."

From that time Kenelm prospered. Eulogistic
letters from the illustrious headmaster showered
in upon Sir Peter.   At the age of sixteen Kenelm
Digby was the head of the school, and quitting
it finally, brought home the following letter from
his Orbilius to Sir Peter, marked 'confidential;'—

"DEAR SIR PETER CHILLINGLY,—I have never
felt more anxious for the future career of any of
my pupils than I do for that of your son. He is
so clever that, with ease to himself, he may be-

come a great man. He is so peculiar, that it is quite as likely that he may only make himself known to the world as a great oddity. That distinguished teacher, Dr. Arnold, said that the difference between one boy and another was not so much talent as energy. Your son has talent, has energy—yet he wants something for success in life; he wants the faculty of amalgamation. He is of a melancholic and therefore unsocial temperament. He will not act in concert with others. He is lovable enough; the other boys like him, especially the smaller ones, with whom he is a sort of hero; but he has not one intimate friend. So far as school learning is concerned, he might go to college at once, and with the certainty of distinction, provided he chose to exert himself. But if I may venture to offer an advice, I should say employ the next two years in letting him see a little more of real life, and acquire a due sense of its practical objects. Send him to a private tutor who is not a pedant, but a man of letters or a man of the world, and if in the metropolis so much the better. In a word, my young friend

is unlike other people; and, with qualities that
might do anything in life, I fear, unless you can
get him to be like other people, that he will do
nothing. Excuse the freedom with which I write,
and ascribe it to the singular interest with which
your son has inspired me.—I have the honour to
be, dear Sir Peter, yours truly,

"WILLIAM HORTON."

Upon the strength of this letter Sir Peter did
not indeed summon another family council; for
he did not consider that his three maiden sisters
could offer any practical advice on the matter.
And as to Mr. Gordon, that gentleman having gone
to law on the great timber question, and having
been signally beaten thereon, had informed Sir
Peter that he disowned him as a cousin and despised him as a man—not exactly in those words
—more covertly, and therefore more stingingly.
But Sir Peter invited Mr. Mivers for a week's
shooting, and requested the Rev. John to meet
him.

Mr. Mivers arrived. The sixteen years that

had elapsed since he was first introduced to the
reader, had made no perceptible change in his
appearance. It was one of his maxims that in
youth a man of the world should appear older
than he is; and in middle age, and thence to his
dying day, younger. And he announced one secret for attaining that art in these words: "Begin
your wig early, thus you never become grey."

Unlike most philosophers, Mivers made his
practice conform to his precepts; and while in
the prime of youth inaugurated a wig in a fashion
that defied the flight of time, not curly and hya-
cinthine, but straight-haired and unassuming. He
looked five-and-thirty from the day he put on
that wig at the age of twenty-five. He looked
five-and-thirty now at the age of fifty-one.

"I mean," said he, "to remain thirty-five all
my life. No better age to stick at. People may
choose to say I am more, but I shall not own it.
No one is bound to criminate himself."

Mr. Mivers had some other aphorisms on this
important subject. One was, "Refuse to be ill.
Never tell people you are ill; never own it to

yourself. Illness is one of those things which a man should resist on principle at the onset. It should never be allowed to get in the thin end of the wedge. But take care of your constitution, and, having ascertained the best habits for it, keep to them like clockwork." Mr. Mivers would not have missed his constitutional walk in the Park before breakfast, if, by going in a cab to St. Giles's, he could have saved the city of London from conflagration.

Another aphorism of his was, "If you want to keep young, live in a metropolis; never stay above a few weeks at a time in the country. Take two men of similar constitution at the age of twenty-five; let one live in London and enjoy a regular sort of club-life; send the other to some rural district, preposterously called 'salubrious.' Look at these men when they have both reached the age of forty-five. The London man has preserved his figure, the rural man has a paunch. The London man has an interesting delicacy of complexion; the face of the rural man is coarse-grained and perhaps jowly."

A third axiom was, "Don't be a family man; nothing ages one like matrimonial felicity and paternal ties. Never multiply cares, and pack up your life in the briefest compass you can. Why add to your carpet-bag of troubles the contents of a lady's imperials and bonnet-boxes, and the travelling *fourgon* required by the nursery. Shun ambition—it is so gouty. It takes a great deal out of a man's life, and gives him nothing worth having till he has ceased to enjoy it."

Another of his aphorisms was this, "A fresh mind keeps the body fresh. Take in the ideas of the day, drain off those of yesterday. As to the morrow, time enough to consider it when it becomes to-day."

Preserving himself by attention to these rules, Mr. Mivers appeared at Exmundham *totus*, *teres*, but not *rotundus*—a man of middle height, slender, upright, with well-cut, small, slight features, thin lips, enclosing an excellent set of teeth, even, white, and not indebted to the dentist. For the sake of those teeth he shunned acid wines, especially hock in all its varieties, culinary sweets, and hot drinks. He drank even his tea cold. "There are," he said, "two things in life that a sage must preserve at every sacrifice, the coats of his stomach and the enamel of his teeth. Some evils admit of consolations: there are no comforters for dyspepsia and toothache." A man of letters, but a man of the world, he had so cultivated his mind as both, that he was feared as the one, and liked as the other. As a man of letters he despised the world; as a man of the world he despised letters. As the representative of both he revered himself.

———

CHAPTER IX.

ON the evening of the third day from the arrival of Mr. Mivers, he, the Parson, and Sir Peter were seated in the host's parlour, the Parson in an arm-chair by the ingle, smoking a short cutty-pipe; Mivers at length on the couch slowly inhaling the perfumes of one of his own choice *trabucos*. Sir Peter never smoked. There were spirits and hot water and lemons on the table. The Parson was famed for skill in the composition of toddy. From time to time the Parson sipped his glass, and Sir Peter, less frequently, did the same. It is needless to say that Mr. Mivers eschewed toddy; but beside him, on a chair, was a tumbler and large carafe of iced water.

SIR PETER.—"Cousin Mivers, you have now had time to study Kenelm, and to compare his

character with that assigned to him in the Doctor's
letter."

MIVERS (languidly).—"Ay."

SIR PETER.—"I ask you, as a man of the
world, what you think I had best do with the boy.
Shall I send him to such a tutor as the Doctor
suggests? Cousin John is not of the same mind
as the Doctor, and thinks that Kenelm's oddities
are fine things in their way, and should not be
prematurely ground out of him by contact with
worldly tutors and London pavements."

"Ay," repeated Mr. Mivers, more languidly
than before. After a pause he added, "Parson
John, let us hear you."

The Parson laid aside his cutty-pipe, and
emptied his fourth tumbler of toddy, then, throw-
ing back his head in the dreamy fashion of the
great Coleridge when he indulged in a mono-
logue, he thus began, speaking somewhat through
his nose—

"At the morning of life——"

Here Mivers shrugged his shoulders, turned

round on his couch, and closed his eyes with the sigh of a man resigning himself to a homily.

"At the morning of life, when the dews——"

"I knew the dews were coming," said Mivers. "Dry them, if you please; nothing so unwholesome. We anticipate what you mean to say, which is plainly this—When a fellow is sixteen he is very fresh; so he is—pass on—what then?"

"If you mean to interrupt me with your habitual cynicism," said the Parson, "why did you ask to hear me?"

"That was a mistake, I grant; but who on earth could conceive that you were going to commence in that florid style. Morning of life indeed!—bosh!"

"Cousin Mivers," said Sir Peter, "you are not reviewing John's style in 'The Londoner;' and I will beg you to remember that my son's morning of life is a serious thing to his father, and not to be nipped in its bud by a cousin. Proceed, John!"

Quoth the Parson, good-humouredly, "I will adapt my style to the taste of my critic. When a fellow is at the age of sixteen, and very fresh to life, the question is whether he should begin thus prematurely to exchange the ideas that belong to youth for the ideas that properly belong to middle age,—whether he should begin to acquire that knowledge of the world which middle-aged men have acquired and can teach. I think not. I would rather have him yet awhile in the company of the poets—in the indulgence of glorious hopes and beautiful dreams, forming to himself some type of the Heroic, which he will keep before his eyes as a standard when he goes into the world as man. There are two schools of thought for the formation of character—the Real and Ideal. I would form the character in the Ideal school, in order to make it bolder and grander and lovelier when it takes its place in that every-day life which is called the Real. And therefore I am not for placing the descendant of Sir Kenelm Digby, in the interval between school and college, with a man of the world, probably as cynical as cousin Mivers, and living in the stony thoroughfares of London."

MR. MIVERS (rousing himself).—"Before we plunge into that Serbonian bog—the controversy between the Realistic and the Idealistic academicians—I think the first thing to decide is what you want Kenelm to be hereafter. When I order a pair of shoes, I decide beforehand what kind of shoes they are to be—court pumps or strong walking-shoes; and I don't ask the shoemaker to give me a preliminary lecture upon the different purposes of locomotion to which leather can be applied. If, Sir Peter, you want Kenelm to scribble lackadaisical poems, listen to Parson John; if you want to fill his head with pastoral rubbish about innocent love, which may end in marrying the Miller's Daughter, listen to Parson John; if you want him to enter life a soft-headed greenhorn, who will sign any bill carrying 50 per cent. to which a young scamp asks him to be security, listen to Parson John; in fine, if you wish a clever lad to become either a pigeon or a ringdove, a credulous booby or a sentimental milksop, Parson John is the best adviser you can have."

5*

"But I don't want my son to ripen into either of those imbecile developments of species."

"Then don't listen to Parson John; and there's an end of the discussion."

"No, there is not. I have not heard your advice what to do if John's advice is not to be taken."

Mr. Mivers hesitated. He seemed puzzled.

"The fact is," said the Parson, "that Mivers got up 'The Londoner' upon a principle that regulates his own mind,—find fault with the way everything is done, but never commit yourself by saying how anything can be done better."

"That is true," said Mivers, candidly. "The destructive order of mind is seldom allied to the constructive. I and 'The Londoner' are destructive by nature and by policy. We can reduce a building into rubbish, but we don't profess to turn rubbish into a building. We are critics, and, as you say, not such fools as to commit ourselves to the proposition of amendments that can be criticised by others. Nevertheless, for your sake, cousin Peter, and on the condition that if I give my advice you will never say that I gave it, and if you take it, that you will never reproach me if it turns out, as most advice does, very ill—I will depart from my custom and hazard my opinion."

"I accept the conditions."

"Well, then, with every new generation there springs up a new order of ideas. The earlier the age at which a man seizes the ideas that will influence his own generation, the more he has a start in the race with his contemporaries. If Kenelm comprehends at sixteen those intellectual signs of the time which, when he goes up to college, he will find young men of eighteen or twenty only just *prepared* to comprehend, he will produce a deep impression of his powers for reasoning, and their adaptation to actual life, which will be of great service to him later. Now the ideas that influence the mass of the rising generation never have their well-head in the generation itself. They have their source in the generation before them, generally in a small minority, neglected or contemned by the great majority which adopt them later. Therefore a lad at the age of sixteen, if he wants to get at such ideas, must come into close contact with some superior mind in which they were conceived twenty or thirty years before. I am consequently for placing Kenelm with a person from whom the new ideas can be learned. I am also for his being placed in the metropolis during the process of this initiation. With such introductions as are at our command, he may come in contact not only with new ideas, but with eminent men in all vocations. It is a great thing to mix betimes with clever people. One picks their brains unconsciously. There is another advantage, and not a small one, in this early entrance into good society. A youth learns manners, self-possession, readiness of resource; and he is much less likely to get into scrapes and contract tastes for low vices and mean dissipation, when he comes into life wholly his own master, after having acquired a predilection for refined companionship, under the guidance of those competent to select it. There, I have talked myself out of breath. And you had better decide at once in favour of my advice; for as I am of a contradictory temperament, myself of to-morrow may probably contradict myself of to-day."

Sir Peter was greatly impressed with his cousin's argumentative eloquence.

The Parson smoked his cutty-pipe in silence until appealed to by Sir Peter, and he then said, "In this programme of education for a Christian gentleman, the part of Christian seems to me left out."

"The tendency of the age," observed Mr. Mivers, calmly, "is towards that omission. Secular education is the necessary reaction from the special theological training which arose in the dislike of one set of Christians to the teaching of another set; and as these antagonists will not agree how religion is to be taught, either there must be no teaching at all, or religion must be eliminated from the tuition."

"That may do very well for some huge system of national education," said Sir Peter, "but it does not apply to Kenelm, as one of a family all of whose members belong to the Established Church. He may be taught the creed of his forefathers without offending a Dissenter."

"Which Established Church is he to belong to?" asked Mr. Mivers,—"High Church, Low Church, Broad Church, Puséyite Church, Ritualistic Church, or any other Established Church that may be coming into fashion?"

"Pshaw!" said the Parson. "That sneer is out of place. You know very well that one merit of our Church is the spirit of toleration, which does not magnify every variety of opinion into a heresy or a schism. But if Sir Peter sends his son at the age of sixteen to a tutor who eliminates the religion of Christianity from his teaching, he deserves to be thrashed within an inch of his life; and," continued the Parson, eyeing Sir Peter sternly, and mechanically turning up his cuffs, "I should *like* to thrash him."

"Gently, John," said Sir Peter, recoiling; "gently, my dear kinsman. My heir shall not be educated as a heathen, and Mivers is only bantering us. Come, Mivers, do you happen to know among your London friends some man who, though a scholar and a man of the world, is still a Christian?"

"A Christian as by law established?"

"Well—yes."

"And who will receive Kenelm as a pupil?"

"Of course I am not putting such questions to you out of idle curiosity."

"I know exactly the man. He was originally intended for orders, and is a very learned theologian. He relinquished the thought of the clerical profession on succeeding to a small landed estate by the sudden death of an elder brother. He then came to London and bought experience—that is, he was naturally generous— he became easily taken in—got into difficulties —the estate was transferred to trustees for the benefit of creditors, and on the payment of £400 a-year to himself. By this time he was married and had two children. He found the necessity of employing his pen in order to add to his income, and is one of the ablest contributors to the periodical press. He is an elegant scholar, an effective writer, much courted by public men, a thorough gentleman, has a pleasant house, and receives the best society. Having been once taken in, he defies any one to take him in again. His experience was not bought too dearly. No more acute and accomplished man of the world. The three hundred a-year or so that you would pay for Kenelm would suit him very well. His name is Welby, and he lives in Chester Square."

"No doubt he is a contributor to 'The Londoner,'" said the Parson, sarcastically.

"True. He writes our classical, theological, and metaphysical articles. Suppose I invite him to come here for a day or two, and you can see him and judge for yourself, Sir Peter?"

"Do."

CHAPTER X.

MR. WELBY arrived, and pleased everybody. A man of the happiest manners, easy and courteous. There was no pedantry in him, yet you could soon see that his reading covered an extensive surface, and here and there had dived deeply. He enchanted the Parson by his comments on St. Chrysostom; he dazzled Sir Peter with his lore in the antiquities of ancient Britain; he captivated Kenelm by his readiness to enter into that most disputatious of sciences called metaphysics; while for Lady Chillingly, and the three sisters who were invited to meet him, he was more entertaining, but not less instructive. Equally at home in novels and in good books, he gave to the spinsters a list of innocent works in either; while for Lady Chillingly he sparkled with anecdotes of fashionable life, the newest *bons mots*, the latest scandals. In fact, Mr. Welby was one of those brilliant per-

sons who adorn any society amidst which they
are thrown. If at heart he was a disappointed
man, the disappointment was concealed by an
even serenity of spirits; he had entertained high
and justifiable. hopes of a brilliant career and a
lasting reputation as a theologian and a preacher;
the succession to his estate at the age of twenty-
three had changed the nature of his ambition.
The charm of his manner was such that he sprang
at once into the fashion, and became beguiled.
by his own genial temperament into that lesser
but pleasanter kind of ambition which contents
itself with social successes, and enjoys the present
hour.   When his circumstances compelled him to
eke out his income by literary profits, he slid
into the grooves of periodical composition, and
resigned all thoughts of the labour required for
any complete work, which might take much time
and be attended with scanty profits. He still
remained very popular in society, and perhaps
his general reputation for ability made him fear-
ful to hazard it by any great undertaking. He
was not, like Mivers, a despiser of all men and

all things; but he regarded men and things as an indifferent though good-natured spectator regards the thronging streets from a drawing-room window. He could not be called *blasé*, but he was thoroughly *désillusionné*. Once over-romantic, his character now was so entirely imbued with the neutral tints of life that romance offended his taste as an obtrusion of violent colour into a sober woof. He was become a thorough Realist in his code of criticism, and in his worldly mode of action and thought. But Parson John did not perceive this, for Welby listened to that gentleman's eulogies on the Ideal school without troubling himself to contradict them. He had grown too indolent to be combative in conversation, and only as a critic betrayèd such pugnacity as remained to him by the polished cruelty of sarcasm.

He came off with flying colours through an examination into his Church orthodoxy instituted by the Parson and Sir Peter. Amid a cloud of ecclesiastical erudition, his own opinions vanished in those of the Fathers. In truth, he was a Realist in religion as in everything else. He regarded Christianity as a type of existent civilisation, which ought to be reverenced, as one might recognise the other types of that civilisation—such as the liberty of the press, the representative system, white neckcloths and black coats of an evening, &c. He belonged, therefore, to what he himself called the school of Eclectical Christiology, and accommodated the reasonings of Deism to the doctrines of the Church, if not as a creed, at least as an institution. Finally, he united all the Chillingly votes in his favour; and when he departed from the Hall, carried off Kenelm for his initiation into the new ideas that were to govern his generation.

CHAPTER XI.

KENELM remained a year and a half with this distinguished preceptor. During that time he learned much in book-lore; he saw much, too, of the eminent men of the day, in literature, the law, and the senate. He saw, also, a good deal of the fashionable world. Fine ladies, who had been friends of his mother in her youth, took him up, counselled and petted him. One in especial, the Marchioness of Glenalvon, to whom he was endeared by grateful association. For her youngest son had been a fellow-pupil of Kenelm's at Merton School, and Kenelm had saved his life from drowning. The poor boy died of consumption later, and her grief for his loss made her affection for Kenelm yet more tender. Lady Glenalvon was one of the queens of the London world. Though in her fiftieth year, she was still very handsome; she was also very accomplished, very clever, and very kind-hearted, as some of such queens are; just one of those women invaluable in forming the manners and elevating the character of young men destined to make a figure in after-life. But she was very angry with herself in thinking that she failed to arouse any such ambition in the heir of the Chillinglys.

It may here be said that Kenelm was not without great advantages of form and countenance. He was tall, and the youthful grace of his proportions concealed his physical strength, which was extraordinary rather from the iron texture than the bulk of his thews and sinews. His face, though it certainly lacked the roundness of youth, had a grave, sombre, haunting sort of beauty, not artistically regular, but picturesque, peculiar, with large dark expressive eyes, and a certain indescribable combination of sweetness and melancholy in his quiet smile. He never laughed audibly, but he had a quick sense of the comic, and his eye would laugh when his lips were silent. He would say queer, droll, unexpected things, which passed for humour; but, save for that gleam in the eye, he could not have said them with more seeming innocence of intentional joke if he had been a monk of La Trappe looking up from the grave he was digging in order to utter "memento mori."

That face of his was a great 'take in.' Women thought it full of romantic sentiment—the face of one easily moved to love, and whose love would be replete alike with poetry and passion. But he remained as proof as the youthful Hippolytus to all female attraction. He delighted the Parson by keeping up his practice in athletic pursuits, and obtained a reputation at the pugilistic school, which he attended regularly, as the best gentleman boxer about town.

He made many acquaintances, but still formed no friendships. Yet every one who saw him much conceived affection for him. If he did not return that affection, he did not repel it. He was exceedingly gentle in voice and manner, and had all his father's placidity of temper—children and dogs took to him as by instinct.

On leaving Mr. Welby's, Kenelm carried to Cambridge a mind largely stocked with the new

ideas that were budding into leaf. He certainly
astonished the other freshmen, and occasionally
puzzled the mighty Fellows of Trinity and St.
John's. But he gradually withdrew himself much
from general society. In fact, he was too old
in mind for his years; and after having mixed in
the choicest circles of a metropolis, college sup-
pers and wine-parties had little charm for him.
He maintained his pugilistic renown; and on
certain occasions, when some delicate undergra-
duate had been bullied by some gigantic barge-
man, his muscular Christianity nobly developed
itself. He did not do as much as he might have
done in the more intellectual ways of academical
distinction. Still, he was always among the first
in the college examinations; he won two university
prizes, and took a very creditable degree, after
which he returned home, more odd, more saturnine—in short, less like other people—than when
he had left Merton School. He had woven a
solitude round him out of his own heart, and in
that solitude he sate still and watchful as a
spider sits in his web.

Whether from natural temperament, or from his educational training under such teachers as Mr. Mivers, who carried out the new ideas of reform by revering nothing in the past, and Mr. Welby, who accepted the routine of the present as realistic, and pooh-poohed all visions of the future as idealistic, Kenelm's chief mental characteristic was a kind of tranquil indifferentism. It was difficult to detect in him either of those ordinary incentives to action—vanity or ambition, the yearning for applause or the desire of power. To all female fascinations he had been hitherto star-proof. He had never experienced love, but he had read a good deal about it, and that passion seemed to him an unaccountable aberration of human reason, and an ignominious surrender of the equanimity of thought which it should be the object of masculine natures to maintain undisturbed. A very eloquent book in praise of celibacy, and entitled "The Approach to the Angels," written by that eminent Oxford scholar, Decimus Roach, had produced so remarkable an effect upon his youthful mind, that, had

he been a Roman Catholic, he might have become a monk. Where he most evinced ardour,
it was a logician's ardour for abstract truth—
that is, for what *he* considered truth; and as
what seems truth to one man is sure to seem
falsehood to some other man, this predilection of
his was not without its inconveniences and dangers, as may probably be seen in the following
chapter.

Meanwhile, rightly to appreciate his conduct
therein, I entreat thee, O candid Reader (not that
any Reader ever is candid), to remember that he
is brimful of new ideas, which, met by a deep
and hostile undercurrent of old ideas, become
more provocatively billowy and surging.

CHAPTER XII.

THERE had been great festivities at Exmundham, in celebration of the honour bestowed upon
the world by the fact that Kenelm Chillingly had
lived twenty-one years in it.

The young heir had made a speech to the as-
sembled tenants and other admitted revellers,
which had by no means added to the exhilaration
of the proceedings. He spoke with a fluency and
self-possession which were surprising in a youth
addressing a multitude for the first time. But his
speech was not cheerful.

The principal tenant on the estate, in propos-
ing his health, had naturally referred to the long
line of his ancestors. His father's merits as man
and landlord had been enthusiastically com-
memorated, and many happy auguries for his
own future career had been drawn, partly from
the excellences of his parentage, partly from his

own youthful promise in the honours achieved at
the university.

Kenelm Chillingly in reply largely availed himself of those new ideas which were to influence
the rising generation, and with which he had been
rendered familiar by the journal of Mr. Mivers
and the conversation of Mr. Welby.

He briefly disposed of the ancestral part of
the question. He observed that it was singular
to note how long any given family or dynasty
could continue to flourish in any given nook of
matter in creation, without any exhibition of intellectual powers beyond those displayed by a
succession of vegetable crops. "It is certainly
true," he said, "that the Chillinglys have lived in
this place from father to son for about a fourth
part of the history of the world, since the date
which Sir Isaac Newton assigns to the Deluge.
But, so far as can be judged by existent records,
the world has not been in any way wiser or better for their existence. They were born to eat as
long as they could eat, and when they could eat
no longer they died. Not that in this respect

they were a whit less insignificant than the generality of their fellow-creatures. Most of us now present," continued the youthful orator, "are only born in order to die; and the chief consolation of our wounded pride in admitting this fact, is in the probability that our posterity will not be of more consequence to the scheme of nature than we ourselves are." Passing from that philosophical view of his own ancestors in particular, and of the human race in general, Kenelm Chillingly then touched with serene analysis on the eulogies lavished on his father as man and landlord.

"As man," he said, "my father no doubt deserves all that can be said by man in favour of man. But what, at the best, is man? A crude, struggling, undeveloped embryo, of whom it is the highest attribute that he feels a vague consciousness that he is only an embryo, and cannot complete himself till he ceases to be a man; that is, until he becomes another being in another form of existence. We can praise a dog as a dog, because a dog is a completed *ens*, and not an embryo. But to praise a man as man, for-

getting that he is only a germ out of which a
form wholly different is ultimately to spring, is
equally opposed to Scriptural belief in his present
crudity and imperfection, and to psychological or
metaphysical examination of a mental construction
evidently designed for purposes that he can never
fulfil as man. That my father is an embryo not
more incomplete than any present, is quite true;
but that, you will see on reflection, is saying very
little on his behalf. Even in the boasted physical
formation of us men, you are aware that the best-
shaped amongst us, according to the last scientific
discoveries, is only a development of some hide-
ous hairy animal, such as a gorilla; and the ancestral gorilla itself had its own aboriginal fore-
father in a small marine animal shaped like a
two-necked bottle. The probability is that, some
day or other, we shall be exterminated by a new
development of species.

"As for the merits assigned to my father as
landlord, I must respectfully dissent from the
panegyrics so rashly bestowed on him. For all
sound reasoners must concur in this, that the

first duty of an owner of land is not to the occupiers to whom he leases it, but to the nation at
large. It is his duty to see that the land yields
to the community the utmost it can yield. In
order to effect this object a landlord should put
up his farms to competition, exacting the highest
rent he can possibly get from responsible compe-
titors. Competitive examination is the enlightened
order of the day, even in professions in which
the best men would have qualities that defy examination. In agriculture, happily, the principle
of competitive examination is not so hostile to
the choice of the best man as it must be, for instance, in diplomacy, where a Talleyrand would
be excluded for knowing no language but his
own; and still more in the army, where promotion
would be denied to an officer who, like Marl-
borough, could not spell. But in agriculture a landlord has only to inquire who can give the highest rent, having the largest capital, subject by the
strictest penalties of law to the conditions of a
lease dictated by the most scientific agriculturists
under penalties fixed by the most cautious con-

veyancers. By this mode of procedure, recom-
mended by the most liberal economists of our
age—barring those still more liberal who deny
that property in land is any property at all—by
this mode of procedure, I say, a landlord does
his duty to his country. He secures tenants who
can produce the most to the community by their
capital, tested through competitive examination
into their bankers' accounts and the security they
can give, and through the rigidity of covenants
suggested by a Liebig and reduced into law by
a Chitty. But on my father's land I see a great
many tenants with little skill and less capital,
ignorant of a Liebig and revolting from a Chitty,
and no filial enthusiasm can induce me honestly
to say that my father is a good landlord. He has
preferred his affection for individuals to his duties
to the community. It is not, my friends, a question whether a handful of farmers like yourselves
go to the workhouse or not. It is a consumer's
question. Do you produce the maximum of corn
to the consumer?

"With respect to myself," continued the orator, warming, as the cold he had engendered in his audience became more freezingly felt—"with respect to myself, I do not deny that, owing to the accident of training for a very faulty and contracted course of education, I have obtained what are called 'honours' at the University of Cambridge; but you must not regard that fact as a promise of any worth in my future passage through life. Some of the most useless persons —especially narrow-minded and bigoted—have acquired far higher honours at the university than have fallen to my lot.

"I thank you no less for the civil things you have said of me and of my family; but I shall endeavour to walk to that grave to which we are all bound with a tranquil indifference as to what people may say of me in so short a journey. And the sooner, my friends, we get to our journey's end, the better our chance of escaping a great many pains, troubles, sins, and diseases. So that when I drink to your good healths, you must feel that in reality I wish you an early deliverance from the ills to which flesh is exposed, and which so generally increase with our years, that good health is scarcely compatible with the decaying faculties of old age.   Gentlemen, your good healths!"

· CHAPTER XIII.

THE morning after these birthday rejoicings, Sir Peter and Lady Chillingly held a long consultation on the peculiarities of their heir, and the best mode of instilling into his mind the expediency either of entertaining more pleasing views, or at least of professing less unpopular sentiments—compatibly of course, though they did not say it, with the new ideas that were to govern his century. Having come to an agreement on this delicate subject, they went forth, arm in arm, in search of their heir. Kenelm seldom met them at breakfast. He was an early riser, and accustomed to solitary rambles before his parents were out of bed.

The worthy pair found Kenelm seated on the banks of a trout-stream that meandered through Chillingly Park, dipping his line into the water, and yawning, with apparent relief in that operation.

"Does fishing amuse you, my boy?" said Sir Peter, heartily.

"Not in the least, sir," answered Kenelm.

"Then why do you do it?" asked Lady Chillingly.

"Because I know nothing else that amuses me more."

"Ah! that is it," said Sir Peter; "the whole secret of Kenelm's oddities is to be found in these words, my dear; he needs amusement. Voltaire says truly, 'amusement is one of the wants of man.' And if Kenelm could be amused like other people, he would be like other people."

"In that case," said Kenelm, gravely, and extracting from the water a small but lively trout, which settled itself in Lady Chillingly's lap—"in that case I would rather not be amused. I have no interest in the absurdities of other people. The instinct of self-preservation compels me to have some interest in my own."

"Kenelm, sir," exclaimed Lady Chillingly,

with an animation into which her tranquil lady-ship was very rarely betrayed, "take away that horrid damp thing! Put down your rod and attend to what your father says. Your strange conduct gives us cause of serious anxiety."

Kenelm unhooked the trout, deposited the fish in his basket, and raising his large eyes to his father's face, said, "What is there in my con-duct that occasions you displeasure?"

"Not displeasure, Kenelm," said Sir Peter, kindly, "but anxiety; your mother has hit upon the right word. You see, my dear son, that it is my wish that you should distinguish yourself in the world. You might represent this county, as your ancestors have done before. I had looked forward to the proceedings of yesterday as an admirable occasion for your introduction to your future constituents. Oratory is the talent most appreciated in a free country, and why should you not be an orator? Demosthenes says that delivery, delivery, delivery, is the art of oratory; and your delivery is excellent, graceful, self-possessed, classical."

"Pardon me, my dear father, Demosthenes does not say delivery, nor action, as the word is commonly rendered; he says, 'acting or stage-play'—ὑπόκρισις; the art by which a man delivers a speech in a feigned character—whence we get the word hypocrisy. Hypocrisy, hypocrisy, hypocrisy! is, according to Demosthenes, the triple art of the orator. Do you wish me to become triply a hypocrite?"

"Kenelm, I am ashamed of you. You know as well as I do that it is only by metaphor that you can twist the word ascribed to the great Athenian into the sense of hypocrisy. But assuming it, as you say, to mean not delivery, but acting, I understand why your *début* as an orator was not successful. Your delivery was excellent, your acting defective. An orator should please, conciliate, persuade, prepossess. You did the reverse of all this; and though you produced a great effect, the effect was so decidedly to your disadvantage, that it would have lost you an election on any hustings in England."

"Am I to understand, my dear father," said

Kenelm, in the mournful and compassionate tones with which a pious minister of the Church reproves some abandoned and hoary sinner—"am I to understand that you would commend to your son the adoption of deliberate falsehood for the gain of a selfish advantage?"

"Deliberate falsehood! you impertinent puppy!"

"Puppy!" repeated Kenelm, not indignantly but musingly—"puppy!—a well-bred puppy takes after its parents."

Sir Peter burst out laughing.

Lady Chillingly rose with dignity, shook her gown, unfolded her parasol, and stalked away speechless.

"Now, look you, Kenelm," said Sir Peter, as soon as he had composed himself. "These quips and humours of yours are amusing enough to an eccentric man like myself, but they will not do for the world; and how at your age, and with the rare advantages you have had in an early introduction to the best intellectual society, under the guidance of a tutor acquainted with the new ideas which are to influence the conduct of statesmen, you could have made so silly a speech as you did yesterday, I cannot understand."

"My dear father, allow me to assure you that the ideas I expressed are the new ideas most in vogue—ideas expressed in still plainer, or, if you prefer the epithet, still sillier terms than I employed. You will find them instilled into the public mind by 'The Londoner,' and by most intellectual journals of a liberal character."

"Kenelm, Kenelm, such ideas would turn the world topsy-turvy."

"New ideas always do tend to turn old ideas topsy-turvy. And the world, after all, is only an idea, which is turned topsy-turvy with every successive century."

"You make me sick of the word ideas. Leave off your metaphysics and study real life."

"It is real life which I did study under Mr. Welby. He is the Archimandrite of Realism. It is sham life which you wish me to study. To oblige you I am willing to commence it. I daresay it is very pleasant. Real life is not; on the contrary—dull." And Kenelm yawned again.

"Have you no young friends among your fellow-collegians?"

"Friends! certainly not, sir. But I believe I have some enemies, who answer the same purpose as friends, only they don't hurt one so much."

"Do you mean to say that you lived alone at Cambridge?"

"No, I lived a good deal with Aristophanes, and a little with Conic Sections and Hydrostatics."

"Books. Dry company."

"Móre innocent, at least, than moist company. Did you ever get drunk, sir?"

"Drunk!"

"I tried to do so once with the young companions whom you would commend to me as friends. I don't think I succeeded, but I woke with a headache. Real life at college abounds with headache."

"Kenelm, my boy, one thing is clear—you must travel."

7*

"As you please, sir. Marcus Antoninus says that it is all one to a stone whether it be thrown upwards or downwards. When shall I start?"

"Very soon. Of course there are preparations to make; you should have a travelling companion. I don't mean a tutor—you are too clever and too steady to need one—but a pleasant, sensible, well-mannered young person of your own age."

"My own age—male or female?"

Sir Peter tried hard to frown. The utmost he could do was to reply gravely, "FEMALE! If I said you were too steady to need a tutor, it was because you have hitherto seemed little likely to be led out of your way by female allurements. Among your other studies may I inquire if you have included that which no man has ever yet thoroughly mastered—the study of woman?"

"Certainly. Do you object to my catching another trout?"

"Trout be——blest, or the reverse. So you have studied woman. I should never have thought it. Where and when did you commence that department of science?"

"When? ever since I was ten years old. Where? first in your own house, then at college. Hush!—a bite," and another trout left its native element and alighted on Sir Peter's nose, whence it was solemnly transferred to the basket.

"At ten years old, and in my own house. That flaunting hussy Jane, the under-housemaid——"

"Jane! No, sir. Pamela, Miss Byron, Clarissa —females in Richardson, who, according to Dr. Johnson, 'taught the passions to move at the command of virtue.' I trust for your sake that Dr. Johnson did not err in that assertion, for I found all these females at night in your own private apartments."

"Oh!" said Sir Peter, "that's all."

"All I remember at ten years old," replied Kenelm.

"And at Mr. Welby's or at college," proceeded Sir Peter, timorously, "was your acquaintance with females of the same kind?"

Kenelm shook his head. "Much worse; they were very naughty indeed at college."

"I should think so, with such a lot of young fellows running after them."

"Very few fellows run after the females I mean—rather avoid them."

"So much the better."

"No, my father, so much the worse; without an intimate knowledge of those females there is little use going to college at all."

"Explain yourself."

"Every one who receives a classical education is introduced into their society—Pyrrha and Lydia, Glycera and Corinna, and many more all of the same sort; and then the females in Aristophanes, what do you say to them, sir?"

"Is it only females who lived 2000 or 3000 years ago, or more probably never lived at all, whose intimacy you have cultivated? Have you never admired any real women?"

"Real women! I never met one. Never met a woman who was not a sham, a sham from the moment she is told to be pretty-behaved, conceal her sentiments, and look fibs when she does not speak them. But if I am to learn sham life, I suppose I must put up with sham women."

"Have you been crossed in love that you speak so bitterly of the sex?"

"I don't speak bitterly of the sex. Examine any woman on her oath, and she'll own she is a sham, always has been, and always will be, and is proud of it."

"I am glad your mother is not by to hear you. You will think differently one of these days. Meanwhile, to turn to the other sex, is there no young man of your own rank with whom you would like to travel?"

"Certainly not. I hate quarrelling."

"As you please. But you cannot go quite alone; I will find you a good travelling servant. I must write to town to-day about your preparations, and in another week or so I hope all will be ready. Your allowance will be whatever you like to fix it at; you have never been extravagant, and—boy—I love you. Amuse yourself, enjoy yourself, and come back cured of your oddities, but preserving your honour."

Sir Peter bent down and kissed his son's brow. Kenelm was moved; he rose, put his arm round his father's shoulder, and lovingly said, in an undertone, "If ever I am tempted to do a base thing, may I remember whose son I am—I shall be safe then." He withdrew his arm as he said this, and took his solitary way along the banks of the stream, forgetful of rod and line.

———

CHAPTER XIV.

THE young man continued to skirt the side of the stream, until he reached the boundary pale of the park. Here, placed on a rough grass mound, some former proprietor, of a social temperament, had built a kind of belvidere, so as to command a cheerful view of the highroad below. Mechanically the heir of the Chillinglys ascended the mound, seated himself within the belvidere, and leant his chin on his hand in a thoughtful attitude. It was rarely that the building was honoured by a human visitor—its habitual occupants were spiders. Of those industrious insects it was a well-populated colony. Their webs, darkened with dust, and ornamented with the wings, and legs, and skeletons of many an unfortunate traveller, clung thick to angle and window-sill, festooned the rickety table on which the young man leant his elbow, and described geometrical circles and rhomboids between the gaping rails that formed the backs of venerable chairs. One large black spider—who was probably the oldest inhabitant, and held possession of the best place by the window, ready to offer perfidious welcome to every winged itinerant who might be tempted to turn aside from the highroad for the sake of a little cool and repose—rushed from its innermost penetralia at the entrance of Kenelm, and remained motionless in the centre of its meshes, staring at him. It did not seem quite sure whether the stranger was too big or not.

"It is a wonderful proof of the wisdom of Providence," said Kenelm, "that whenever any large number of its creatures forms a community or class, a secret element of disunion enters into the hearts of the individuals forming the congregation, and prevents their co-operating heartily and effectually for their common interest. 'The fleas would have dragged me out of bed if they had been unanimous,' said the great Mr. Curran: and there can be no doubt that if all the spiders in this commonwealth would unite to attack me in a body, I should fall a victim to their combined nippers. But spiders, though inhabiting the same region, constituting the same race, animated by the same instincts, do not combine even against a butterfly; each seeks his own special advantage, and not that of the community at large. And how completely the life of each thing resembles a circle in this respect, that it can never touch another circle at more than one point. Nay, I doubt if it quite touches it even there,—there is a space between every atom—self is always selfish; and yet there are eminent masters in the Academe of New Ideas who wish to make us believe that all the working classes of a civilised world could merge every difference pf race, creed, intellect, individual propensities and interests, into the construction of a single web, stocked as a larder in common!" Here the soliloquist came to a dead stop, and leaning out of the window, contemplated the highroad. It was a very fine highroad—straight and level, kept in excellent order by turnpikes at every eight miles. A plea-

sant greensward bordered it on either side, and
under the belvidere the benevolence of some
mediæval Chillingly had placed a little drinking
fountain for the refreshment of wayfarers. Close
to the fountain stood a rude stone bench, overshadowed by a large willow, and commanding
from the high table-ground on which it was
placed a wide view of corn-fields, meadows, and
distant hills, suffused in the mellow light of the
summer sun. Along that road there came suc-
cessively a waggon filled with passengers seated
on straw—an old woman, a pretty girl, two
children; then a stout farmer going to market in
his dog-cart; then three flies carrying fares to the
nearest railway station; then a handsome young
man on horseback, a handsome young lady by
his side, a groom behind. It was easy to see
that the young man and young lady were lovers.
See it in his ardent looks and serious lips parted
but for whispers only to be heard by her;—see
it in her downcast eyes and heightened colour.
"'Alas! regardless of their doom,'" muttered
Kenelm, "what trouble those 'little victims' are

preparing for themselves and their progeny! Would
I could lend them Decimus Roach's 'Approach
to the Angels!'" The road now for some minutes
became solitary and still, when there was heard
to the right a sprightly sort of carol, half sung,
half recited, in musical voice, with a singularly
clear enunciation, so that the words reached
Kenelm's ear distinctly.   They ran thus:—

> "Black Karl looked forth from his cottage-door,
>   He looked on the forest green ;
> And down the path, with his dogs before,
>   Came the Ritter of Neirestein :
> Singing—singing—lustily singing,
>   Down the path, with his dogs before,
> Came the Ritter of Neirestein."

At a voice so English, attuned to a strain so
Germanic, Kenelm pricked up attentive ears, and,
turning his eye down the road, beheld, emerging
from the shade of beeches that overhung the
park pales, a figure that did not altogether
harmonise with the idea of a Ritter of Neirestein.
It was, nevertheless, a picturesque figure enough.
The man was attired in a somewhat threadbare
suit of Lincoln green, with a high-crowned Tyrolese

hat; a knapsack was slung behind his shoulders, and he was attended by a white Pomeranian dog, evidently foot-sore, but doing his best to appear proficient in the chase by limping some yards in advance of his master, and sniffing into the hedges for rats and mice, and such small deer.

By the time the pedestrian had reached to the close of his refrain he had gained the fountain, and greeted it with an exclamation of pleasure. Slipping the knapsack from his shoulder, he filled the iron ladle attached to the basin. He then called to the dog by the name of Max, and held the ladle for him to drink. Not till the animal had satisfied his thirst did the master assuage his own. Then, lifting his hat and bathing his temples and face, the pedestrian seated himself on the bench, and the dog nestled on the turf at his feet. After a little pause the wayfarer began again, though in a lower and slower tone, to chant his refrain, and proceeded, with abrupt snatches, to link the verse on to another stanza. It was evident that he was either endeavouring to remember or to invent, and it seemed rather like the latter and more laborious operation of mind.

"'Why on foot, why on foot, Ritter Karl,' quoth he,
　'And not on thy palfrey grey?'

Palfrey grey—hum—grey.

'The run of ill-luck was too strong for me,
　And has galloped my steed away.'

That will do—good!"

"Good indeed! He is easily satisfied," muttered Kenelm. "But such pedestrians don't pass the road every day. Let us talk to him." So saying he slipped quietly out of the window, descended the mound, and letting himself into the road by a screened wicket-gate, took his noiseless stand behind the wayfarer and beneath the bowery willow.

The man had now sunk into silence. Perhaps he had tired himself of rhymes; or perhaps the mechanism of verse-making had been replaced by that kind of sentiment, or that kind of reverie, which is common to the temperaments of those who indulge in verse-making. But the loveliness of the scene before him had caught his eye and fixed it into an intent gaze upon wooded land-scapes stretching farther and farther to the range of hills on which the heaven seemed to rest.

"I should like to hear the rest of that German ballad," said a voice, abruptly.

The wayfarer started, and turning round, pre-sented to Kenelm's view a countenance in the ripest noon of manhood, with locks and beard of a deep rich auburn, bright blue eyes, and a wonderful nameless charm both of feature and expression, very cheerful, very frank, and not without a certain nobleness of character which seemed to exact respect.

"I beg your pardon for my interruption," said Kenelm, lifting his hat; "but I overheard you reciting; and though I suppose your verses are a translation from the German, I don't re-member anything like them in such popular German poets as I happen to have read."

"It is not a translation, sir," replied the itinerant. "I was only trying to string together some ideas that came into my head this fine morning."

"You are a poet, then?" said Kenelm, seating himself on the bench.

"I dare not say poet. I am a verse-maker."

"Sir, I know there is a distinction. Many poets of the present day, considered very good, are uncommonly bad verse-makers. For my part, I could more readily imagine them to be good poets if they did not make verses at all. But can I not hear the rest of the ballad?"

"Alas! the rest of the ballad is not yet made. It is rather a long subject, and my flights are very brief."

"That is much in their favour, and very unlike the poetry in fashion. You do not belong, I think, to this neighbourhood. Are you and your dog travelling far?"

"It is my holiday time, and I ramble on through the summer. I am travelling far, for I travel till September. Life amid summer fields is a very joyous thing."

"Is it indeed?" said Kenelm, with much

naïveté. "I should have thought that, long before September, you would have got very much
bored with the fields and the dog and yourself
altogether.   But, to be sure, you have the
resource of verse-making, and that seems a very
pleasant and absorbing occupation to those who
practise it—from our old friend Horace, knead-
ing laboured Alcaics into honey in his summer
rambles among the watered woodlands of Tibur,
to Cardinal Richelieu employing himself on
French rhymes in the intervals between chopping
off noblemen's heads.   It does not seem to
signify much whether the verses be good or bad,
so far as the pleasure of the verse-maker himself
is concerned; for Richelieu was as much charmed
with his occupation as Horace was, and his verses
were certainly not Horatian."

"Surely at your age, sir, and with your evident
education——"

"Say culture; that's the word in fashion
nowadays."

"—Well, your evident culture—you must
have made verses."

"Latin verses—yes—and occasionally Greek, I was obliged to do so at school. It did not amuse me."

"Try English."

Kenelm shook his head. "Not I. Every cobbler should stick to his last."

"Well, put aside the verse-making: don't you find a sensible enjoyment in those solitary summer walks, when you have Nature all to yourself—enjoyment in marking all the mobile, evanescent changes in her face—her laugh, her smile, her tears, her very frown!"

"Assuming that by Nature you mean a mechanical series of external phenomena, I object to your speaking of a machinery as if it were a person of the feminine gender—*her* laugh, *her* smile, &c. As well talk of the laugh and smile of a steam-engine. But to descend to common-sense. I grant there is some pleasure in solitary rambles in fine weather and amid varying scenery. You say that it is a holiday excursion that you are enjoying: I presume, therefore, that you have some practical occupation which consumes the time that you do not devote to a holiday?"

"Yes; I am not altogether an idler. I work sometimes, though not so hard as I ought. 'Life is earnest,' as the poet says. But I and my dog are rested now, and as I have still a long walk before me, I must wish you good-day."

"I fear," said Kenelm, with a grave and sweet politeness of tone and manner, which he could command at times, and which, in its difference from merely conventional urbanity, was not without fascination—"I fear that I have offended you by a question that must have seemed to you inquisitive—perhaps impertinent; accept my excuse; it is very rarely that I meet any one who interests me; and you do." As he spoke he offered his hand, which the wayfarer shook very cordially.

"I should be a churl indeed if your question could have given me offence. It is rather perhaps I who am guilty of impertinence, if I take advantage of my seniority in years, and tender you a counsel. Do not despise Nature, or regard her as a steam-engine; you will find in her a very agreeable and conversable friend, if you will cultivate her intimacy. And I don't know a better mode of doing so at your age, and with your strong limbs, than putting a knapsack on your shoulders, and turning foot-traveller, like myself."

"Sir, I thank you for your counsel; and I trust we may meet again, and interchange ideas as to the thing you call Nature—a thing which science and art never appear to see with the same eyes. If to an artist Nature has a soul, why, so has a steam-engine. Art gifts with soul all matter that it contemplates; science turns all that is already gifted with soul into matter. Good-day, sir."

Here Kenelm turned back abruptly, and the traveller went his way, silently and thoughtfully.

CHAPTER XV.

KENELM retraced his steps homeward under the shade of his 'old hereditary trees.' One might have thought his path along the green-swards, and by the side of the babbling rivulet, was pleasanter and more conducive to peaceful thoughts than the broad, dusty thoroughfare along which plodded the wanderer he had quitted. But the man addicted to reverie forms his own landscapes and colours his own skies.

"It is," soliloquised Kenelm Chillingly, "a strange yearning I have long felt—to get out of myself—to get, as it were, into another man's skin—and have a little variety of thought and emotion. One's self is always the same self; and that is why I yawn so often. But if I can't get into another man's skin, the next best thing is to get as unlike myself as I possibly can do. Let me see what is myself. Myself is Kenelm Chillingly, son and heir to a rich gentleman. But a

fellow with a knapsack on his back, sleeping at
wayside inns, is not at all like Kenelm Chillingly
—especially if he is very short of money, and
may come to want a dinner. Perhaps that sort
of fellow may take a livelier view of things: he
can't take a duller one. Courage, Myself,—you
and I can but try."

For the next two days Kenelm was observed
to be unusually pleasant. He·yawned much less
frequently, walked with his father, played piquet
with his mother, was more like other people.
Sir Peter was charmed; he ascribed this happy
change to the preparations he was making for
Kenelm's travelling in style. The proud father
was in active correspondence with his great
London friends, seeking letters of introduction
to Kenelm for all the courts of Europe. Port-
manteaus, with every modern convenience, were
ordered; an experienced courier, who could talk
all languages—and cook French dishes if required
—was invited to name his terms. In short, every
arrangement worthy a young patrician's entrance
into the great world was in rapid progress, when

suddenly Kenelm Chillingly disappeared, leaving behind him on Sir Peter's library-table the following letter:—

"My very dear Father,— Obedient to your desire, I depart in search of real life and real persons, or of the best imitations of them. Forgive me, I beseech you, if I commence that search in my own way. I have seen enough of ladies and gentlemen for the present—they must be all very much alike in every part of the world. You desired me to be amused. I go to try if that be possible. Ladies and gentlemen are not amusing; the more lady-like or gentleman-like they are, the more insipid I find them. My dear father, I go in quest of adventure like Amadis of Gaul, like Don Quixote, like Gil Blas, like Roderick Random—like, in short, the only real people seeking real life—the people who never existed except in books. I go on foot, I go alone. I have provided myself with a larger amount of money than I ought to spend, because every man must buy experience, and the first fees are heavy.

In fact, I have put fifty pounds into my pocket-book and into my purse five sovereigns and seventeen shillings. This sum ought to last me a year, but I daresay inexperience will do me out of it in a month, so we will count it as nothing. Since you have asked me to fix my own allowance, I will beg you kindly to commence it this day in advance, by an order to your banker to cash my cheques to the amount of five pounds, and to the same amount monthly—viz., at the rate of sixty pounds a-year. With that sum I can't starve, and if I want more it may be amusing to work for it. Pray don't send after me, or institute inquiries, or disturb the household, and set all the neighbourhood talking, by any mention either of my project or of your surprise at it. I will not fail to write to you from time to time.

"You will judge best what to say to my dear mother. If you tell her the truth, which of course I should do did I tell her anything, my request is virtually frustrated, and I shall be the talk of the county. You, I know, don't think telling fibs is immoral, when it happens to be convenient, as it would be in this case.

"I expect to be absent a year or eighteen months; if I prolong my travels it shall be in the way you proposed. I will then take my place in polite society, call upon you to pay all expenses, and fib on my own account to any extent required by that world of fiction which is peopled by illusions and governed by shams.

"Heaven bless you, my dear father, and be quite sure that if I get into any trouble requiring a friend, it is to you I shall turn. As yet I have no other friend on earth, and with prudence and good-luck I may escape the infliction of any other friend.—Yours ever affectionately,

KENELM.

"*P.S.*—Dear father, I open my letter in your library to say again 'Bless you,' and to tell you how fondly I kissed your old beaver gloves, which I found on the table."

When Sir Peter came to that postscript he

took off his spectacles and wiped them—they were very moist.

Then he fell into a profound meditation. Sir Peter was, as I have said, a learned man; he was also in some things a sensible man; and he had a strong sympathy with the humorous side of his son's crotchety character. What was to be said to Lady Chillingly? That matron was quite guiltless of any crime which should deprive her of a husband's confidence in a matter relating to her only son. She was a virtuous matron—morals irreproachable — manners dignified, and *she-baronety*. Any one seeing her for the first time would intuitively say, "Your ladyship." Was this a matron to be suppressed in any well-ordered domestic circle? Sir Peter's conscience loudly answered, "No;" but when, putting conscience into his pocket, he regarded the question at issue as a man of the world, Sir Peter felt that to communicate the contents of his son's letter to Lady Chillingly would be the foolishest thing he could possibly do. Did she know that Kenelm had absconded with the family dignity invested in his very

name, no marital authority short of such abuses of
power as constitute the offence of cruelty in a
wife's action for divorce from social board and
nuptial bed, could prevent Lady Chillingly from
summoning all the grooms, sending them in all
directions, with strict orders to bring back the
runaway dead or alive—the walls would be placarded with handbills, "Strayed from his home,"
&c.,—the police would be telegraphing private
instructions from town to town — the scandal
would stick to Kenelm Chillingly for life, accompanied with vague hints of criminal propensities
and insane hallucinations — he would be ever
afterwards pointed out as "THE MAN WHO HAD
DISAPPEARED." And to disappear and to turn up
again, instead of being murdered, is the most
hateful thing a man can do; all the newspapers
bark at him, 'Tray, Blanche, Sweetheart, and all;'
strict explanations of the unseemly fact of his
safe existence are demanded in the name of
public decorum, and no explanations are accepted—it is life saved, character lost.

Sir Peter seized his hat and walked forth, not

to deliberate whether to fib or not to fib to the wife of his bosom, but to consider what kind of fib would the most quickly sink into the bosom of his wife.

A few turns to and fro the terrace sufficed for the conception and maturing of the fib selected; a proof that Sir Peter was a practised fibber. He re-entered the house, passed into her ladyship's habitual sitting-room, and said, with careless gaiety, "My old friend the Duke of Clareville is just setting off on a tour to Switzerland with his family. His youngest daughter, Lady Jane, is a pretty girl, and would not be a bad match for Kenelm."

"Lady Jane, the youngest daughter with fair hair, whom I saw last as a very charming child, nursing a lovely doll presented to her by the Empress Eugénie. A good match indeed for Kenelm."

"I am glad you agree with me. Would it not be a favourable step towards that alliance, and an excellent thing for Kenelm generally, if he were to visit the Continent as one of the Duke's travelling party?"

"Of course it would."

"Then you approve what I have done—the Duke starts the day after to-morrow, and I have packed Kenelm off to town, with a letter to my old friend.   You will excuse all leave-taking. You know that though the best of sons he is an odd fellow; and seeing that I had talked him into it, I struck while the iron was hot, and sent him off by the express at nine o'clock this morning, for fear that if I allowed any delay he would talk himself out of it."

"Do you mean to say Kenelm is actually gone?   Good gracious!"

Sir Peter stole softly from the room, and summoning his valet, said, "I have sent Mr. Chillingly to London.   Pack up the clothes he is likely to want, so that he can have them sent at once, whenever he writes for them."

And thus by a judicious violation of truth on the part of his father, that exemplary truth-teller Kenelm Chillingly saved the honour of his house and his own reputation from the breath of scandal and the inquisition of the police.   He was not "THE MAN WHO HAD DISAPPEARED."

BOOK II.

CHAPTER I.

KENELM CHILLINGLY had quitted the paternal home at daybreak before any of the household was astir.

"Unquestionably," said he, as he walked along the solitary lanes—"unquestionably I begin the world as poets begin poetry, an imitator and a plagiarist. I am imitating an itinerant verse-maker, as, no doubt, he began by imitating some other maker of verse. But if there be anything in me, it will work itself out in original form. And after all, the verse-maker is not the inventor of ideas. Adventure on foot is a notion that remounts to the age of fable. Hercules, for instance,—that was the way in which he got to heaven, as a foot-traveller. How solitary the world is at this hour! Is it not for that reason that this is of all hours the most beautiful?"

Here he paused, and looked around and above. It was the very height of summer. The sun was just rising over gentle sloping uplands. All the dews on the hedgerows sparkled. There was not a cloud in the heavens. Uprose from the green blades of the corn a solitary skylark. His voice woke up the other birds. A few minutes more, and the joyous concert began. Kenelm reverently doffed his hat and bowed his head in mute homage and thanksgiving.

———————

CHAPTER II.

ABOUT nine o'clock Kenelm entered a town some twelve miles distant from his father's house, and towards which he had designedly made his way, because in that town he was scarcely if at all known by sight, and he might there make the purchases he required without attracting any marked observation. He had selected for his travelling costume a shooting-dress, as the simplest and least likely to belong to his rank as a gentleman. But still in its very cut there was an air of distinction, and every labourer he had met on the way had touched his hat to him. Besides, who wears a shooting-dress in the middle of June, or a shooting-dress at all, unless he be either a gamekeeper or a gentleman licensed to shoot?

Kenelm entered a large store-shop for ready-made clothes, and purchased a suit, such as might be worn on Sundays by a small country yeoman or tenant-farmer of a petty holding,—a stout coarse broadcloth upper garment, half coat, half jacket, with waistcoat to match, strong corduroy trousers, a smart Belcher neckcloth, with a small stock of linen and woollen socks in harmony with the other raiment. He bought also a leathern knapsack, just big enough to contain this wardrobe, and a couple of books, which, with his combs and brushes, he had brought away in his pockets. For among all his trunks at home there was no knapsack.

These purchases made and paid for, he passed quickly through the town, and stopped at a humble inn at the outskirts, to which he was attracted by the notice, "Refreshment for man and beast." He entered a little sanded parlour, which at that hour he had all to himself, called for breakfast, and devoured the best part of a fourpenny loaf, with a couple of hard eggs.

Thus recruited, he again sallied forth, and deviating into a thick wood by the roadside, he exchanged the habiliments with which he had left home for those he had purchased, and by the help of one or two big stones sunk the relinquished garments into a small but deep pool which he was lucky enough to find in a bush-grown dell much haunted by snipes in the winter.

"Now," said Kenelm, "I really begin to think I have got out of myself. I am in another man's skin; for what, after all, is a skin but a soul's clothing, and what is clothing but a decenter skin? Of its own natural skin every civilised soul is ashamed. It is the height of impropriety for any one but the lowest kind of savage to show it. If the purest soul now existent upon earth, the Pope of Rome's or the Archbishop of Canterbury's, were to pass down the Strand with the skin which nature gave to it bare to the eye, it would be brought up before a magistrate, prosecuted by the Society for the Suppression of Vice, and committed to jail as a public nuisance.

"Decidedly I am now in another man's skin. Kenelm Chillingly, I no longer

Remain

Yours faithfully;

But am,

With profound consideration,

Your obedient humble Servant."

9*

With light step and elated crest, the wanderer, thus transformed, sprang from the wood into the dusty thoroughfare.

He had travelled on for about an hour, meeting but few other passengers, when he heard to the right a loud shrill young voice, "Help, help! —I will not go—I tell you, I will not!" Just before him stood, by a high five-barred gate, a pensive grey cob attached to a neat-looking gig. The bridle was loose on the cob's neck. The animal was evidently accustomed to stand quietly when ordered to do so, and glad of the opportunity.

The cries, "Help, help!" were renewed, mingled with louder tones in a rougher voice, tones of wrath and menace. Evidently these sounds did nót come from the cob. Kenelm looked over the gate, and saw a few yards distant, in a grass field, a well-dressed boy struggling violently against a stout middle-aged man who was rudely hauling him along by the arm.

The chivalry natural to a namesake of the valiant Sir Kenelm Digby was instantly aroused.

He vaulted over the gate, seized the man by the collar, and exclaimed, "For shame! what are you doing to that poor boy?—let him go!"

"Why the devil do you interfere?" cried the stout man—his eyes glaring and his lips foaming with rage. "Ah, are you the villain?—yes, no doubt of it. I'll give it to you, jackanapes," and still grasping the boy with one hand, with the other the stout man darted a blow at Kenelm, from which nothing less than the practised pugilistic skill and natural alertness of the youth thus suddenly assaulted could have saved his eyes and nose. As it was, the stout man had the worst of it; the blow was parried, returned with a dexterous manœuvre of Kenelm's right foot in Cornish fashion, and *procumbit humi bos* —the stout man lay sprawling on his back. The boy, thus released, seized hold of Kenelm by the arm, and hurrying him along up the field, cried, "Come, come before he gets up! save me! save me!" Ere he had recovered his own surprise, the boy had dragged Kenelm to the gate, and jumped into the gig, sobbing forth, "Get in, get in. I can't drive; get in, and drive—you. Quick! quick!"

"But," began Kenelm.

"Get in, or I shall go mad." Kenelm obeyed, the boy gave him the reins, and seizing the whip himself, applied it lustily to the cob. On sprang the cob. "Stop—stop—stop, thief!— villain!—Holloa!—thieves—thieves—thieves!— stop!" cried a voice behind. Kenelm involuntarily turned his head and beheld the stout man perched upon the gate and gesticulating furiously. It was but a glimpse; again the whip was plied, the cob frantically broke into a gallop, the gig jolted and bumped and swerved, and it was not till they had put a good mile between themselves and the stout man that Kenelm succeeded in obtaining possession of the whip, and calming the cob into a rational trot.

"Young gentleman," then said Kenelm, "perhaps you will have the goodness to explain."

"By-and-by; get on, that's a good fellow; you shall be well paid for it—well and handsomely."

Quoth Kenelm, gravely, "I know that in real life payment and service naturally go together. But we will put aside the payment till you tell me what is to be the service. And first, whither am I to drive you? We are coming to a place where three roads meet; which of the three shall I take?"

"Oh, I don't know; there is a finger-post. I want to get to—but it is a secret; you'll not betray me. Promise—swear."

"I don't swear except when I am in a passion, which, I am sorry to say, is very seldom; and I don't promise till I know what I promise; neither do I go on driving runaway boys in other men's gigs unless I know that I am taking them to a safe place, where their papas and mammas can get at them."

"I have no papa, no mamma," said the boy dolefully, and with quivering lips.

"Poor boy. I suppose that burly brute is your schoolmaster, and you are running away home for fear of a flogging."

The boy burst out laughing; a pretty silvery

merry laugh, it thrilled through Kenelm Chillingly. "No, he would not flog me; he is not a schoolmaster; he is worse than that."

"Is it possible? What is he?"

"An uncle."

"Hum! uncles are proverbial for cruelty; were so in the classical days, and Richard III. was the only scholar in his family."

"Eh! classical and Richard III.!" said the boy, startled, and looking attentively at the pensive driver. "Who are you? you talk like a gentleman."

"I beg pardon. I'll not do so again if I can help it." "Decidedly," thought Kenelm, "I am beginning to be amused. What a blessing it is to get into another man's skin, and another man's gig too!" Aloud, "Here we are at the finger-post. If you are running away from your uncle, it is time to inform me where you are running to."

Here the boy leaned over the gig and examined the finger-post. Then he clapped his hands joyfully.

"All right! I thought so—'To Tor-Hadham, eighteen miles.' That's the road to Tor-Hadham."

"Do you mean to say I am to drive you all that way—eighteen miles?"

"Yes."

"And to whom are you going?"

"I will tell you by-and-by. Do go on—do, pray. I can't drive—never drove in my life—or I would not ask you. Pray, pray, don't desert me! If you are a gentleman you will not; and if you are not a gentleman, I have got £10 in my purse, which you shall have when I am safe at Tor-Hadham. Don't hesitate; my whole life is at stake!" And the boy began once more to sob.

Kenelm directed the pony's head towards Tor-Hadham, and the boy ceased to sob.

"You are a good, dear fellow," said the boy, wiping his eyes. "I am afraid I am taking you very much out of your road."

"I have no road in particular, and would as soon go to Tor-Hadham, which I have never seen, as anywhere else. I am but a wanderer on the face of the earth."

"Have you lost your papa and mamma too? Why, you are not much older than I am."

"Little gentleman," said Kenelm, gravely, "I am just of age; and you, I suppose, are about fourteen."

"What fun!" cried the boy, abruptly. "Isn't it fun?"

"It will not be fun if I am sentenced to penal servitude for stealing your uncle's gig, and robbing his little nephew of £10. By the by, that choleric relation of yours meant to knock down somebody else when he struck at me. He asked, 'Are *you* the villain?' Pray who is the villain? he is evidently in your confidence."

"Villain! he is the most honourable, high-minded—— But no matter now; I'll introduce you to him when we reach Tor-Hadham. Whip that pony; he is crawling."

"It is up-hill; a good man spares his beast."

No art and no eloquence could extort from

his young companion any further explanation
than Kenelm had yet received; and indeed, as
the journey advanced, and they approached their
destination, both parties sank into silence. Kenelm
was seriously considering that his first day's experience of real life in the skin of another had
placed in some peril his own. He had knocked
down a man evidently respectable and well to
do, had carried off that man's nephew, and made
free with that man's goods and chattels—*i. e.*, his
gig and horse. All this might be explained satis-
factorily to a justice of the peace, but how? By
returning to his former skin; by avowing himself
to be Kenelm Chillingly, a distinguished university
medalist, heir to no ignoble name and some
£ 10,000 a-year. But then what a scandal! he
who abhorred scandal; in vulgar parlance, what
a "row!" he who denied that the very word
"row" was sanctioned by any classic authorities
in the English language. He would have to explain how he came to be found disguised, carefully disguised, in garments such as no baronet's
eldest son—even though that baronet be the

least ancestral man of mark whom it suits the
convenience of a First Minister to recommend to
the Sovereign for exaltation over the rank of
Mister—was ever beheld in, unless he had taken
flight to the gold-diggings. Was this a position
in which the heir of the Chillinglys, a distinguished family, whose coat of arms dated from
the earliest authenticated period of English
heraldry under Edward III. as Three Fishes
azur, could be placed without grievous slur
on the cold and ancient blood of the Three
Fishes?

And then individually to himself, Kenelm,
irrespectively of the Three Fishes. What a humilia-
tion! He had put aside his respected father's
deliberate preparations for his entrance into real
life; he had perversely chosen his own walk on
his own responsibility; and here, before half the
first day was over, what an infernal scrape he
had walked himself into! And what was his excuse? A wretched little boy, sobbing and chuck-
ling by turns, and yet who was clever enough to
twist Kenelm Chillingly round his finger; twist

him—a man who thought himself so much wiser than his parents—a man who had gained honours at the University—a man of the gravest temperament—a man of so nicely a critical turn of mind that there was not a law of art or nature in which he did not detect a flaw,—that he should get himself into this mess was, to say the least of it, an uncomfortable reflection.

The boy himself, as Kenelm glanced at him from time to time, became impish and Will-of-the-Wisp-ish. Sometimes he laughed to himself loudly, sometimes he wept to himself quietly; sometimes, neither laughing nor weeping, he seemed absorbed in reflection. Twice as they came nearer to the town of Tor-Hadham, Kenelm nudged the boy, and said, "My boy, I must talk with you;" and twice the boy, withdrawing his arm from the nudge, had answered dreamily,

"Hush! I am thinking."

And so they entered the town of Tor-Hadham; the cob very much done up.

.

CHAPTER III.

"Now, young sir," said Kenelm, in a tone calm, but peremptory—"now we are in the town, where am I to take you? and wherever it be, there to say good-bye."

"No, not good-bye. Stay with me a little bit. I begin to feel frightened, and I am so friendless;" and the boy, who had before resented the slightest nudge on the part of Kenelm, now wound his arm into Kenelm's, and clung to him caressingly.

I don't know what my readers have hitherto thought of Kenelm Chillingly, but amid all the curves and windings of his whimsical humour, there was one way that went straight to his heart —you had only to be weaker than himself, and ask his protection.

He turned round abruptly; he forgot all the strangeness of his position, and replied: "Little brute that you are, I'll be shot if I forsake you if in trouble. But some compassion is also due to the cob—for his sake say where we are to stop."

"I'm sure I can't say; I never was here before. Let us go to a nice quiet inn. Drive slowly— we'll look out for one."

Tor-Hadham was a large town, not nominally the capital of the county, but in point of trade, and bustle, and life, virtually the capital. The straight street, through which the cob went as slowly as if he had been drawing a Triumphal Car up the Sacred Hill, presented an animated appearance. The shops had handsome façades and plate-glass windows; the pavements exhibited a lively concourse, evidently not merely of business, but of pleasure, for a large proportion of the passers-by was composed of the fair sex, smartly dressed, many of them young, and some pretty. In fact a regiment of Her Majesty's —th Hussars had been sent into the town two days before, and between the officers of that fortunate regiment, and the fair sex in that hospitable town, there was a natural emulation which should make the greater number of slain and wounded. The advent of these heroes, professional subtracters from hostile, and multipliers of friendly, populations, gave a stimulus to the caterers for those amusements which bring young folks together— archery-meetings, rifle-shootings, concerts, balls, announced in bills attached to boards and walls, and exposed at shop-windows.

The boy looked .eagerly forth from the gig, scanning especially these advertisements, till at length he uttered an excited exclamation, "Ah, I was right—there it is!"

"There what is?" asked Kenelm. "The Inn?" His companion did not answer, but Kenelm following the boy's eyes perceived an immense hand-bill.

"To-morrow Night Theatre opens. Richard III. Mr. Compton."

"Do just ask where the theatre is," said the boy, in a whisper, turning away his head.

Kenelm stopped the cob, made the inquiry,

and was directed to take the next turning to the right. In a few minutes the compo portico of an ugly dilapidated building, dedicated to the Dramatic Muses, presented itself at the angle of a dreary deserted lane. The walls were placarded with play-bills, in which the name of Compton stood forth as gigantic as capitals could make it. The boy drew a sigh. "Now," said he, "let us look out for an inn near here—the nearest."

No inn, however, beyond the rank of a small and questionable-looking public-house, was apparent, until at a distance somewhat remote from the theatre, and in a quaint, old-fashioned, deserted square, a neat newly-whitewashed house displayed upon its frontispiece, in large black letters of funereal aspect, "Temperance Hotel."

"Stop," said the boy; "don't you think that would suit us? it looks quiet."

"Could not look more quiet if it were a tombstone," replied Kenelm.

The boy put his hand upon the reins and stopped the cob. The cob was in that condition that the slightest touch sufficed to stop him, though he turned his head somewhat ruefully, as if in doubt whether hay and corn would be within the regulations of a Temperance Hotel. Kenelm descended and entered the house. A tidy woman emerged from a sort of glass cupboard which constituted the bar, minus the comforting drinks associated with the *beau idéal* of a bar, but which displayed instead two large decanters of cold water with tumblers *à discretion*, and sundry plates of thin biscuits and sponge-cakes. This tidy woman politely inquired what was his "pleasure."

"Pleasure," answered Kenelm, with his usual gravity, "is not the word I should myself have chosen. But could you oblige my horse—I mean *that* horse—with a stall and a feed of oats; and that young gentleman and myself with a private room and a dinner?"

"Dinner!" echoed the hostess—"dinner!"

"A thousand pardons, ma'am. But if the word 'dinner' shock you I retract it, and would say instead, 'something to eat and drink.'"

"Drink! This is strictly a Temperance Hotel, sir."

"Oh, if you don't eat and drink here," exclaimed Kenelm, fiercely, for he was famished, "I wish you good-morning."

"Stay a bit, sir. We do eat and drink here. But we are very simple folks. We allow no fermented liquors."

"Not even a glass of beer?"

"Only ginger-beer. Alcohols are strictly forbidden. We have tea, and coffee, and milk. But most of our customers prefer the pure liquid. As for eating, sir,—anything you order, in reason."

Kenelm shook his head and was retreating, when the boy, who had sprung from the gig and overheard the conversation, cried, petulantly, "What does it signify? Who wants fermented liquors? Water will do very well. And as for dinner,—anything convenient. Please, ma'am, show us into a private room; I am so tired." The last words were said in a caressing manner, and so prettily, that the hostess at once changed

her tone, and muttering, "poor boy!" and, in a
still more subdued mutter, "what a pretty face he
has!" nodded, and led the way up a very clean
old-fashioned staircase.

"But the horse and gig—where are they to
go?" said Kenelm, with a pang of conscience on
reflecting how ill treated hitherto had been both
horse and owner.

"Oh, as for the horse and gig, sir, you will
find Jukes's livery-stables a few yards farther
down. We don't take in horses ourselves—our
customers seldom keep them; but you will find
the best of accommodation at Jukes's."

Kenelm conducted the cob to the livery-
stables thus indicated, and waited to see him
walked about to cool, well rubbed down, and
made comfortable over half a peck of oats—for
Kenelm Chillingly was a humane man to the
brute creation—and then, in a state of ravenous
appetite, returned to the Temperance Hotel, and
was ushered into a small drawing-room, with a
small bit of carpet in the centre, six small chairs
with cane seats, prints on the walls descriptive of

the various effects of intoxicating liquors upon sundry specimens of mankind—some resembling ghosts, others fiends, and all with a general aspect of beggary and perdition, contrasted by Happy-Family pictures—smiling wives, portly husbands, rosy infants, emblematic of the beatified condition of members of the Temperance Society.

A table with a spotless cloth, and knives and forks for two, chiefly, however, attracted Kenelm's attention.

The boy was standing by the window, seemingly gazing on a small aquarium which was there placed, and contained the usual variety of small fishes, reptiles, and insects, enjoying the pleasures of Temperance in its native element, including, of course, an occasional meal upon each other.

"What are they going to give us to eat?" inquired Kenelm. "It must be ready by this time I should think."

Here he gave a brisk tug at the bell-pull. The boy advanced from the window, and as he did so Kenelm was struck with the grace of his

bearing and the improvement in his looks, now
that he was without his hat, and rest and ablu-
tion had refreshed from heat and dust the delicate
bloom of his complexion.   There was no doubt
about it that he was an exceedingly pretty boy,
and if he lived to be a man would make many
a lady's heart ache.   It was with a certain air of
gracious superiority such as is seldom warranted
by superior rank if it be less than royal, and
chiefly becomes a marked seniority in years, that
this young gentleman, approaching the solemn
heir of the Chillinglys, held out his hand and
said—

"Sir, you have behaved extremely well, and
I thank you very much."

"Your Royal Highness is condescending to
say so," replied Kenelm Chillingly, bowing low;
"but have you ordered dinner? and what are
they going to give us?   No one seems to answer
the bell here.   As it is a Temperance Hotel, probably all the servants are drunk."

"Why should they be drunk at a Temperance
Hotel?"

"Why! because, as a general rule, people who flagrantly pretend to anything, are the reverse of that which they pretend to. A man who sets up for a saint is sure to be a sinner, and a man who boasts that he is a sinner, is sure to have some feeble, maudlin, snivelling bit of saintship about him which is enough to make him a humbug. Masculine honesty, whether it be saint-like or sinner-like, does not label itself either saint or sinner. Fancy St. Augustin labelling himself saint, or Robert Burns sinner; and therefore, though, little boy, you have probably not read the Poems of Robert Burns, and have certainly not read the Confessions of St. Augustin, take my word for it, that both those personages were very good fellows; and with a little difference of training and experience, Burns might have written the Confessions, and Augustin the Poems. Powers above! I am starving. What did you order for dinner, and when is it to appear?"

. The boy, who had opened to an enormous width a naturally large pair of hazel eyes, while his tall companion in fustian trousers and Belcher neckcloth spoke thus patronisingly of Robert Burns and St. Augustin, now replied with rather a deprecatory and shamefaced aspect, "I am sorry I was not thinking of dinner. I was not so mindful of you as I ought to have been. The landlady asked me what we would have. I said, 'What you like;' and the landlady muttered something about"——(here the boy hesitated)

"Yes. About what? Mutton-chops?"

"No. Cauliflowers and rice-pudding."

Kenelm Chillingly never swore, never raged. Where ruder beings of human mould swore or raged, he vented displeasure in an expression of countenance so pathetically melancholic and lugubrious that it would have melted the heart of an Hyrcanian tiger. He turned his countenance now on the boy, and murmuring "Cauliflower!—Starvation!" sank into one of the cane-bottomed chairs, and added quietly, "so much for human gratitude!"

The boy was evidently smitten to the heart by the bitter sweetness of this reproach. There were almost tears in his voice, as he said falteringly, "Pray forgive me, I *was* ungrateful. I'll run down and see what there is;" and suiting the action to the word, he disappeared.

Kenelm remained motionless; in fact he was plunged into one of those reveries, or rather absorptions of inward and spiritual being, into which it is said that the consciousness of the Indian Dervish can be, by prolonged fasting, preternaturally resolved. The appetite of all men of powerful muscular development is of a nature far exceeding the properties of any reasonable number of cauliflowers and rice-puddings to satisfy. Witness Hercules himself, whose cravings for substantial nourishment were the standing joke of the classic poets. I don't know that Kenelm Chillingly would have beaten the Theban Hercules either in fighting or in eating; but when he wanted to fight or when he wanted to eat, Hercules would have had to put forth all his strength not to be beaten.

After ten minutes' absence, the boy came back radiant. He tapped Kenelm on the shoulder, and said playfully, "I made them cut a whole loin into chops, besides the cauliflower, and such a big rice-pudding, and eggs and bacon too. Cheer up! it will be served in a minute."

"A—h!" said Kenelm.

"They are good people; they did not mean to stint you; but most of their customers, it seems, live upon vegetables and farinaceous food. There is a society here formed upon that principle; the landlady says they are philosophers!"

At the word 'philosophers' Kenelm's crest rose as that of a practised hunter at the cry of 'Yoiks! Tally-ho!' "Philosophers!" said he— "philosophers indeed! O ignoramuses, who do not even know the structure of the human tooth! Look you, little boy, if nothing were left on this earth of the present race of man, as we are assured upon great authority will be the case one of these days—and a mighty good riddance it will be—if nothing, I say, of man were left except fossils of his teeth and his thumbs, a philosopher of that superior race which will succeed to man would at once see in those relics all his characteristics and all his history; would say, comparing his thumb with the talons of an eagle, the claws of a tiger, the hoof of a horse, the owner of that thumb must have been lord over creatures with talons and claws and hoofs. You may say the monkey tribe has thumbs. True; but compare an ape's thumb with a man's,— could the biggest ape's thumb have built Westminster Abbey? But even thumbs are trivial evidence of man as compared with his teeth. Look at his teeth!"—here Kenelm expanded his jaws from ear to ear and displayed semicircles of ivory, so perfect for the purposes of mastication that the most artistic dentist might have despaired of his power to imitate them— "look, I say, at his teeth!" The boy involuntarily recoiled. "Are the teeth those of a miserable cauliflower-eater? or is it purely by farinaceous food that the proprietor of teeth like man's obtains the rank of the sovereign destroyer of creation? No, little boy, no," continued Kenelm, closing his jaws, but advancing upon the in-

fant, who at each stride receded towards the
aquarium—"no; man is the master of the world,
because of all created beings he devours the
greatest variety and the greatest number of created
things. His teeth evince that man can live upon
every soil from the torrid to the frozen zone, because man can eat everything that other creatures cannot eat. And the formation of his teeth
proves it. A tiger can eat a deer—so can man;
but a tiger can't eat an eel—man can. An
elephant can eat cauliflowers and rice-pudding—
so can man; but an elephant can't eat a beefsteak—man can. In sum, man can live every-
where, because he can eat anything, thanks to his
dental formation!" concluded Kenelm, making a
prodigious stride towards the boy. "Man, when
everything else fails him, eats his own species."

"Don't; you frighten me," said the boy.
"Aha!" clapping his hands with a sensation of
gleeful relief, "here come the mutton-chops!"

A wonderfully clean, well-washed, indeed
well-washed-out, middle-aged parlour-maid now
appeared, dish in hand. Putting the dish on the

table and taking off the cover, the handmaiden
said civilly, though frigidly, like one who lived
upon salad and cold water, "Mistress is sorry to
have kept you waiting, but she thought you were
Vegetarians."

After helping his young friend to a mutton-
chop Kenelm helped himself, and replied, gravely,
"Tell your mistress that if she had only given us
vegetables, I should have eaten you. Tell her
that though man is partially graminivorous, he is
principally carnivorous. Tell her that though a
swine eats cabbages and suchlike, yet where a
swine can get a baby, it eats the baby. Tell
her," continued Kenelm (now at his third chop),
"that there is no animal that in digestive organs
more resembles man than a swine. Ask her if
there is any baby in the house; if so, it would
be safe for the baby to send up some more chops."

As the acutest observer could rarely be quite
sure when Kenelm Chillingly was in jest or in
earnest, the parlour-maid paused a moment and
attempted a pale smile. Kenelm lifted his dark
eyes, unspeakably sad and profound, and said,

mournfully, "I should be so sorry for the baby. Bring the chops!" The parlour-maid vanished. The boy laid down his knife and fork, and looked fixedly and inquisitively on Kenelm. Kenelm, unheeding the look, placed the last chop on the boy's plate.

"No more," cried the boy, impulsively, and returned the chop to the dish. "I have dined—I have had enough."

"Little boy, you lie," said Kenelm; "you have not had enough to keep body and soul together. Eat that chop, or I shall thrash you; whatever I say, I do."

Somehow or other the boy felt quelled; he ate the chop in silence; again looked at Kenelm's face, and said to himself, "I am afraid."

The parlour-maid here entered with a fresh supply of chops and a dish of bacon and eggs, soon followed by a rice-pudding baked in a tin dish, and of size sufficient to have nourished a charity school. When the repast was finished, Kenelm seemed to forget the dangerous properties of the carnivorous animal; and stretching himself indolently out, appeared to be as innocently ruminative as the most domestic of animals graminivorous.

Then said the boy, rather timidly, "May I ask you another favour?"

"Is it to knock down another uncle, or to steal another gig and cob?"

"No, it is very simple: it is merely to find out the address of a friend here; and when found to give him a note from me."

"Does the commission press? 'After dinner rest a while,' saith the proverb; and proverbs are so wise that no one can guess the author of them. They are supposed to be fragments of the philosophy of the antediluvians—came to us packed up in the ark."

"Really, indeed," said the boy, seriously. "How interesting! No, my commission does not press for an hour or so. Do you think, sir, they had any drama before the Deluge?"

"Drama! not a doubt of it. Men who lived one or two thousand years had time to invent and improve everything; and a play could have had its natural length then. It would not have been necessary to crowd the whole history of Macbeth, from his youth to his old age, into an absurd epitome of three hours. One cannot trace a touch of real human nature in any actor's delineation of that very interesting Scotchman, because the actor always comes on the stage as if he were the same age when he murdered Duncan, and when, in his sear and yellow leaf, he was lopped off by Macduff."

"Do you think Macbeth was young when he murdered Duncan?"

"Certainly. No man ever commits a first crime of violent nature, such as murder, after thirty; if he begins before, he may go on up to any age. But youth is the season for commencing those wrong calculations which belong to irrational hope and the sense of physical power. You thus read in the newspapers that the persons who murder their sweethearts are generally from two to six and twenty; and persons who murder from other motives than love—that is, from revenge, avarice, or ambition—are generally about twenty-eight—Iago's age. Twenty-eight is the usual close of the active season for getting rid of one's fellow-creatures—a prize-fighter falls off after that age. I take it that Macbeth was about twenty-eight when he murdered Duncan, and from about fifty-four to sixty when he began to whine about missing the comforts of old age. But can any audience understand that difference of years in seeing a three-hours' play; or does any actor ever pretend to impress it on the audience, and appear as twenty-eight in the first act and a sexagenarian in the fifth?"

"I never thought of that," said the boy, evidently interested. "But I never saw Macbeth. I have seen Richard III.—is not that nice? Don't you dote on the Play? I do. What a glorious life an actor's must be!"

Kenelm, who had been hitherto rather talking to himself than to his youthful companion, here roused his attention, looked on the boy intently, and said—

"I see you are stage-stricken. You have run away from home in order to turn player, and I should not wonder if this note you want me to give is for the manager of the theatre or one of his company."

The young face that encountered Kenelm's dark eye became very flushed, but set and *défiant* in its expression.

"And what if it were—would not you give it?"

"What! help a child of your age, run away from his home, to go upon the stage against the consent of his relations—certainly not."

"I am not a child; but that has nothing to do with it. I don't want to go on the stage, at all events without the consent of the person who has a right to dictate my actions. My note is not to the manager of the theatre, nor to one of his company, but it is to a gentleman who condescends to act here for a few nights—a thorough gentleman—a great actor—my friend, the only friend I have in the world. I say frankly I have run away from home so that he may have that note, and if you will not give it some one else will!"

The boy had risen while he spoke, and he stood erect beside the recumbent Kenelm, his lips quivering, his eyes suffused with suppressed tears, but his whole aspect resolute and determined. Evidently, if he did not get his own way in this world, it would not be for want of will.

"I will take your note," said Kenelm.

"There it is; give it into the hands of the person it is addressed to—Mr. Herbert Compton."

CHAPTER IV.

KENELM took his way to the theatre, and inquired of the doorkeeper for Mr. Herbert Compton. That functionary replied, "Mr. Compton does not act to-night, and is not in the house."

"Who does he lodge?"

The doorkeeper pointed to a grocer's shop on the other side of the way, and said, tersely, "There, private door—knock and ring."

Kenelm did as he was directed. A slatternly maid-servant opened the door, and, in answer to his interrogatory, said that Mr. Compton was at home, but at supper.

"I am sorry to disturb him," said Kenelm, raising his voice, for he heard a clatter of knives and plates within a room hard by at his left, "but my business requires to see him forthwith;" and pushing the maid aside, he entered at once the adjoining banquet-hall.

Before a savoury stew smelling strongly of onions sate a man very much at his ease, without coat or neckcloth, a decidedly handsome man—his hair cut short and his face closely shaven, as befits an actor who has wigs and beards of all hues and forms at his command. The man was not alone; opposite to him sate a lady, who might be a few years younger, of a somewhat faded complexion, but still pretty, with good stage features and a profusion of blond ringlets.

"Mr. Compton, I presume," said Kenelm, with a solemn bow.

"My name is Compton: any message from the theatre? or what do you want with me?"

"I?—nothing!" replied Kenelm; and then deepening his naturally mournful voice into tones ominous and tragic, continued—"By whom you are wanted let this explain;" therewith he placed in Mr. Compton's hand the letter with which he was charged, and stretching his arms and interlacing his fingers in the *pose* of Talma as Julius Cæsar, added, "'*Qu'en dis tu, Brute?*'"

Whether it was from the sombre aspect and
awe-inspiring delivery, or ὑπόχρισις, of the messenger, or the sight of the handwriting on the
address of the missive, Mr. Compton's countenance
suddenly fell, and his hand rested irresolute, as if
not daring to open the letter.

"Never mind me, dear," said the lady with
blond ringlets, in a tone of stinging affability;
"read your *billet-doux;* don't keep the young man
waiting, love!"

"Nonsense, Matilda, nonsense! *billet-doux* indeed! more likely a bill from Duke the tailor.
Excuse me for a moment, my dear. Follow me,
sir," and rising, still with shirt-sleeves uncovered,
he quitted the room, closing the door after him,
motioned Kenelm into a small parlour on the
opposite side of the passage, and by the light of
a suspended gas-lamp ran his eye hastily over
the letter, which, though it seemed very short,
drew from him sundry exclamations. "Good
heavens! how very absurd! what's to be done?"
Then, thrusting the letter into his trousers-pocket,
he fixed upon Kenelm a very brilliant pair of

dark eyes, which soon dropped before the steadfast look of that saturnine adventurer.

"Are you in the confidence of the writer of this letter?" asked Mr. Compton, rather confusedly.

"I am not the confidant of the writer," answered Kenelm, "but for the time being I am the protector!"

"Protector?"

"Protector."

Mr. Compton again eyed the messenger, and this time fully realising the gladiatorial development of that dark stranger's physical form, he grew many shades paler, and involuntarily retreated towards the bell-pull.

After a short pause, he said, "I am requested to call on the writer. If I do so, may I understand that the interview will be strictly private?"

"So far as I am concerned, yes — on the condition that no attempt be made to withdraw the writer from the house."

"Certainly not—certainly not; quite the contrary," exclaimed Mr. Compton, with genuine animation. "Say I will call in half an hour."

"I will give your message," said Kenelm, with a polite inclination of his head; "and pray pardon me if I remind you that I styled myself the protector of your correspondent, and if the slightest advantage be taken of that correspondent's youth and inexperience, or the smallest encouragement be given to plans of abduction from home and friends, the stage will lose an ornament, and Herbert Compton vanish from the scene." With those words Kenelm left the player standing aghast. Gaining the street-door, a lad with a bandbox ran against him and was nearly upset.

"Stupid," cried the lad, "can't you see where you are going? Give this to Mrs. Compton."

"I should deserve the title you give if I did for nothing the business for which you are paid," replied Kenelm, sententiously, and striding on.

CHAPTER V.

"I HAVE fulfilled my mission," said Kenelm, on rejoining his travelling companion. "Mr. Compton said he would be here in half an hour."

"You saw him?"

"Of course; I promised to give your letter into his own hands."

"Was he alone?"

"No; at supper with his wife."

"His wife? what do you mean, sir?—wife! he has no wife."

"Appearances are deceitful. At least he was with a lady who called him 'dear' and 'love' in as spiteful a tone of voice as if she had been his wife; and as I was coming out of his street-door a lad who ran against me asked me to give a bandbox to Mrs. Compton."

The boy turned as white as death, staggered back a few steps, and dropped into a chair.

A suspicion which, during his absence, had suggested itself to Kenelm's inquiring mind, now took strong confirmation. He approached softly, drew a chair close to the companion whom fate had forced upon him, and said in a gentle whisper—

"This is no boy's agitation. If you have been deceived or misled, and I can in any way advise or aid you, count on me as women under the circumstances count on men and gentlemen."

The boy started to his feet, and paced the room with disordered steps, and a countenance working with passions which he attempted vainly to suppress. Suddenly arresting his steps, he seized Kenelm's hand, pressed it convulsively, and said, in a voice struggling against a sob—

"I thank you—I bless you. Leave me now— I would be alone. Alone, too, I must face this man. There may be some mistake yet;—go."

"You will promise not to leave the house till I return?"

"Yes, I promise that."

"And if it be as I fear, you will then let me counsel with and advise you?"

"Heaven help me, if so! Whom else should I trust to? Go—go!"

Kenelm once more found himself in the streets, beneath the mingled light of gas-lamps and the midsummer moon. He walked on mechanically till he reached the extremity of the town. There he halted, and seating himself on a milestone, indulged in these meditations:—

"Kenelm, my friend, you are in a still worse scrape than I thought you were an hour ago. You have evidently now got a woman on your hands. What on earth are you to do with her? A runaway woman, who, meaning to run off with somebody else—such are the crosses and contradictions in human destiny—has run off with you instead. What mortal can hope to be safe? The last thing I thought could befall me when I got up this morning was that I should have any trouble about the other sex before the day was over. If I were of an amatory temperament, the

Fates might have some justification for leading
me into this snare, but, as it is, those meddling
old maids have none. Kenelm, my friend, do
you think you ever can be in love? and, if you
were in love, do you think you could be a
greater fool than you are now?"

Kenelm had not decided this knotty question
in the conference held with himself, when a light
and soft strain of music came upon his ear. It
was but from a stringed instrument, and might
have sounded thin and tinkling, but for the still-
ness of the night, and that peculiar addition of
fulness which music acquires when it is borne
along a tranquil air. Presently a voice in song
was heard from the distance accompanying the
instrument. It was a man's voice, a mellow and
a rich voice, but Kenelm's ear could not catch
the words. Mechanically he moved on towards
the quarter from which the sounds came, for
Kenelm Chillingly had music in his soul, though.
he was not quite aware of it himself. He saw
before him a patch of greensward, on which
grew a solitary elm with a seat for wayfarers

beneath it. From this sward the ground receded
in a wide semicircle bordered partly by shops,
partly by the tea-gardens of a pretty cottage-like
tavern. Round the tables scattered throughout
the gardens were grouped quiet customers, evidently belonging to the class of small trades-
people or superior artisans. They had an appearance of decorous respectability, and were
listening intently to the music. So were many
persons at the shop-doors, and at the windows
of upper rooms. On the sward, a little in advance of the tree, but beneath its shadow, stood
the musician, and in that musician Kenelm recognised the wanderer from whose talk he had
conceived the idea of the pedestrian excursion
which had already brought him into a very awkward position. The instrument on which the
singer accompanied himself was a guitar, and his
song was evidently a love-song, though, as it was
now drawing near to its close, Kenelm could but
imperfectly guess at its general meaning. He
heard enough to perceive that its words were at
least free from the vulgarity which generally

characterises street ballads, and were yet simple enough to please a very homely audience.

When the singer ended there was no applause; but there was evident sensation among the audience—a feeling as if something that had given a common enjoyment had ceased. Presently the white Pomeranian dog, who had hitherto kept himself out of sight under the seat of the elm-tree, advanced, with a small metal tray between his teeth, and, after looking round him deliberately as if to select whom of the audience should be honoured with the commencement of a general subscription, gravely approached Kenelm, stood on his hind-legs, stared at him, and presented the tray.

Kenelm dropped a shilling into that depository, and the dog, looking gratified, took his way towards the tea-gardens.

Lifting his hat, for he was, in his way, a very polite man, Kenelm approached the singer, and, trusting to the alteration in his dress for not being recognised by a stranger who had only once before encountered him, he said—

"Judging by the little I heard, you sing very well, sir. May I ask who composed the words?"

"They are mine," replied the singer.

"And the air?"

"Mine too."

"Accept my compliments. I hope you find these manifestations of genius lucrative?"

The singer, who had not hitherto vouchsafed more than a careless glance at the rustic garb of the questioner, now fixed his eyes full upon Kenelm, and said, with a smile, "Your voice betrays you, sir. We have met before."

"True; but I did not then notice your guitar, nor, though acquainted with your poetical gifts, suppose that you selected this primitive method of making them publicly known."

"Nor did I anticipate the pleasure of meeting you again in the character of Hobnail. Hist! let us keep each other's secret. I am known hereabouts by no other designation than that of the 'Wandering Minstrel.'"

"It is in the capacity of minstrel that I address you. If it be not an impertinent question, do you know any songs which take the other side of the case?"

"What case? I don't understand you, sir."

"The song I heard seemed in praise of that sham called love. Don't you think you could say something more new and more true, treating that aberration from reason with the contempt it deserves?"

"Not if I am to get my travelling expenses paid."

"What! the folly is so popular?"

"Does not your own heart tell you so?"

"Not a bit of it—rather the contrary. Your audience at present seem folks who live by work, and can have little time for such idle phantasies —for, as it is well observed by Ovid, a poet who wrote much on that subject, and professed the most intimate acquaintance with it, 'Idleness is the parent of love.' Can't you sing something in praise of a good dinner? Everybody who works hard has an appetite for food."

The singer again fixed on Kenelm his inquiring eye, but not detecting a vestige of humour in the grave face he contemplated, was rather puzzled how to reply, and therefore remained silent.

"I perceive," resumed Kenelm, "that my observations surprise you: the surprise will vanish on reflection. It has been said by another poet, more reflective than Ovid, 'that the world is governed by love and hunger.' But hunger certainly has the lion's share of the government; and if a poet is really to do what he pretends to do—viz., represent nature—the greater part of his lays should be addressed to the stomach." Here, warming with his subject, Kenelm familiarly laid his hand on the musician's shoulder, and his voice took a tone bordering on enthusiasm. "You will allow that a man, in the normal condition of health, does not fall in love every day. But in the normal condition of health he is hungry every day. Nay, in those early years when you poets say he is most prone to love, he is so especially disposed to hunger that less than three meals a-day can scarcely satisfy his appetite. You may imprison a man for

months, for years, nay, for his whole life—from
infancy to any age which Sir Cornewall Lewis
may allow him to attain—without letting him be
in love at all. But if you shut him up for a
week without putting something into his stomach,
you will find him at the end of it as dead as a
door-nail."

Here the singer, who had gradually retreated
before the energetic advance of the orator, sank
into the seat by the elm-tree, and said, pathetically,
"Sir, you have fairly argued me down. Will you
please to come to the conclusion which you de-
duce from your premises?"

"Simply this, that where you find one human
being who cares about love, you will find a thousand susceptible to the charms of a dinner; and
if you wish to be the popular minnesinger or
troubadour of the age, appeal to nature, sir—
appeal to nature; drop all hackneyed rhapsodies
about a rosy cheek, and strike your lyre to the
theme of a beefsteak."

The dog had for some minutes regained his
master's side, standing on his hind-legs, with the

tray, tolerably well filled with copper coins, between his teeth; and now, justly aggrieved by the
inattention which detained him in that arti-
ficial attitude, dropped the tray and growled at
Kenelm.

At the same time there came an impatient
sound from the audience in the tea-garden. They
wanted another song for their money.

The singer rose, obedient to the summons.
"Excuse me, sir; but I am called upon to——"

"To sing again?"

"Yes."

"And on the subject I suggest?"

"No, indeed."

"What! love, again?"

"I am afraid so."

"I wish you good-evening, then. You seem
a well-educated man—more shame to you. Perhaps we may meet once more in our rambles,
when the question can be properly argued out."

Kenelm lifted his hat, and turned on his heel.
Before he reached the street, the sweet voice of

the singer again smote his ears; but the only word distinguishable in the distance, ringing out at the close of the refrain, was "love."

"Fiddle-de-dee," said Kenelm.

CHAPTER VI.

As Kenelm regained the street dignified by the edifice of the Temperance Hotel, a figure, dressed picturesquely in a Spanish cloak, brushed hurriedly by him, but not so fast as to be unrecognised as the tragedian. "Hem!" muttered Kenelm—"I don't think there is much triumph in that face. I suspect he has been scolded."

The boy—if Kenelm's travelling companion is still to be so designated—was leaning against the mantelpiece as Kenelm re-entered the dining-room. There was an air of profound dejection about the boy's listless attitude and in the drooping tearless eyes.

"My dear child," said Kenelm, in the softest tones of his plaintive voice, "do not honour me with any confidence that may be painful. But let me hope that you have dismissed for ever all thoughts of going on the stage."

"Yes," was the scarce audible answer.

"And now only remains the question, 'What is to be done?'"

"I am sure I don't know, and I don't care."

"Then you leave it to me to know and to care, and assuming for the moment as a fact, that which is one of the greatest lies in this mendacious world—namely, that all men are brothers, you will consider me as an elder brother, who will counsel and control you as he would—an imprudent young——sister. I see very well how it is. Somehow or other you, having first admired Mr. Compton as Romeo or Richard III., made his acquaintance as Mr. Compton. He allowed you to believe him a single man. In a romantic moment you escaped from your home, with the design of adopting the profession of the stage, and of becoming Mrs. Compton."

"Oh," broke out the girl, since her sex must now be declared—"oh," she exclaimed, with a passionate sob, "what a fool I have been! Only do not think worse of me than I deserve. The man did deceive me; he did not think I should take him at his word, and follow him here, or his wife would not have appeared. I should not have known he had one; and—and——" here her voice was choked under her passion.

"But now you have discovered the truth, let us thank heaven that you are saved from shame and misery. I must despatch a telegram to your uncle—give me his address."

"No, no."

"There is not a 'No' possible in this case, my child. Your reputation and your future must be saved. Leave me to explain all to your uncle. He is your guardian. I must send for him; nay, nay, there is no option. Hate me now for enforcing your will, you will thank me hereafter. And listen, young lady; if it does pain you to see your uncle, and encounter his reproaches, every fault must undergo its punishment. A brave nature undergoes it cheerfully, as a part of atonement. You are brave. Submit, and in submitting rejoice!"

There was something in Kenelm's voice and manner at once so kindly and so commanding,

that the wayward nature he addressed fairly suc-
cumbed. She gave him her uncle's address,
"John Bovill, Esq., Oakdale, near Westmere." And
after giving it, fixed her eyes mournfully upon
her young adviser, and said with a simple, dreary
pathos, "Now, will you esteem me more, or rather
despise me less?"

She looked so young, nay, so childlike, as she
thus spoke, that Kenelm felt a parental inclination
to draw her on his lap and kiss away her tears.
But he prudently conquered that impulse, and
said, with a melancholy half-smile—

"If human beings despise each other for being young and foolish, the sooner we are exterminated by that superior race which is to succeed
us on earth the better it will be. Adieu till your
uncle comes."

"What! you leave me here—alone?"

"Nay, if your uncle found me under the same
roof, now that I know you are his niece, don't you
think he would have a right to throw me out of
the window? Allow me to practise for myself the
prudence I preach to you. Send for the landlady

to show you your room, shut yourself in there, go to bed, and don't cry more than you can help."

Kenelm shouldered the knapsack he had deposited in a corner of the room, inquired for the telegraph office, despatched a telegram to Mr. Bovill, obtained a bedroom at the Commercial Hotel, and fell asleep muttering these sensible words—

"Rochefoucauld was perfectly right when he said, 'Very few people would fall in love if they had not heard it so much talked about.'"

CHAPTER VII.

KENELM CHILLINGLY rose with the sun, according to his usual custom, and took his way to the Temperance Hotel. All in that sober building seemed still in the arms of Morpheus. He turned towards the stables in which he had left the grey cob, and had the pleasure to see that ill-used animal in the healthful process of rubbing down.

"That's right," said he to the ostler. "I am glad to see you are so early a riser."

"Why," quoth the ostler, "the gentleman as owns the pony knocked me up at two o'clock in the morning, and pleased enough he was to see the creature again lying down in the clean straw."

"Oh, he has arrived at the hotel, I presume? —a stout gentleman?"

"Yes, stout enough; and a passionate gentleman too. Came in a yellow and two posters, knocked up the Temperance, and then knocked up me to see for the pony, and was much put out as he could not get any grog at the Temperance."

"I daresay he was. I wish he had got his grog; it might have put him in better humour. Poor little thing!" muttered Kenelm, turning away; "I am afraid she is in for a regular vituperation. My turn next, I suppose. But he must be a good fellow to have come at once for his niece in the dead of the night."

About nine o'clock Kenelm presented himself again at the Temperance Hotel, inquired for Mr. Bovill, and was shown by the prim maid-servant into the drawing-room, where he found Mr. Bovill seated amicably at breakfast with his niece, who, of course, was still in boy's clothing, having no other costume at hand. To Kenelm's great relief, Mr. Bovill rose from the table with a beaming countenance, and, extending his hand to Kenelm, said—

"Sir, you are a gentleman; sit down, sit down, and take breakfast."

Then, as soon as the maid was out of the room, the uncle continued—

"I have heard all your good conduct from this young simpleton. Things might have been worse, sir."

Kenelm bowed his head, and drew the loaf towards him in silence. Then considering that some apology was due to his entertainer, he said—

"I hope you forgive me for that unfortunate mistake, when——"

"You knocked me down, or rather tripped me up. All right now. Elsie, give the gentleman a cup of tea. Pretty little rogue, is not she? and a good girl, in spite of her nonsense. It was all my fault letting her go to the play and be intimate with Miss Lockit, a stage-stricken, foolish old maid, who ought to have known better than lead her into all this trouble."

"No, uncle," cried the girl, resolutely; "don't blame her, nor any one but me."

Kenelm turned his dark eyes approvingly towards the girl, and saw that her lips were firmly set; there was an expression, not of grief nor shame, but compressed resolution in her countenance. But when her eyes met his they fell softly, and a blush mantled over her cheeks up to her very forehead.

"Ah!" said the uncle, "just like you, Elsie; always ready to take everybody's fault on your own shoulders. Well, well, say no more about that.—Now, my young friend, what brings you across the country tramping it on foot, eh? a young man's whim?" As he spoke, he eyed Kenelm very closely, and his look was that of an intelligent man not unaccustomed to observe the faces of those he conversed with. In fact a more shrewd man of business than Mr. Bovill is seldom met with on 'Change or in market.

"I travel on foot to please myself, sir," answered Kenelm, curtly, and unconsciously set on his guard.

"Of course you do," cried Mr. Bovill, with a jovial laugh. "But it seems you don't object to

a chaise and pony whenever you can get them
for nothing—ha, ha!—excuse me—a joke."

Herewith Mr. Bovill, still in excellent good-
humour, abruptly changed the conversation to
general matters—agricultural prospects—chance
of a good harvest—corn trade—money market in
general—politics—state of the nation.   Kenelm
felt there was an attempt to draw him out, to
sound, to pump him, and replied only by mono-
syllables, generally significant of ignorance on the
questions broached; and at the close, if the philosophical heir of the Chillinglys was in the habit
of allowing himself to be surprised he would certainly have been startled when Mr. Bovill rose,
slapped him on the shoulder, and said in a tone
of great satisfaction, "Just as I thought, sir; you
know nothing of these matters—you are a gentleman born and bred—your clothes can't disguise
you, sir. Elsie was right. My dear, just leave us
for a few minutes; I have something to say to
our young friend. You can get ready meanwhile
to go with me."   Elsie left the table and walked
obediently towards the doorway. There she halted

a moment, turned round, and looked timidly towards Kenelm. He had naturally risen from his seat as she rose, and advanced some paces as if to open the door for her. Thus their looks encountered. He could not interpret that shy gaze of hers; it was tender, it was deprecating, it was humble, it was pleading; a man accustomed to female conquests might have thought it was something more, something in which was the key to all. But that something more was an unknown tongue to Kenelm Chillingly.

When the two men were alone, Mr. Bovill reseated himself and motioned to Kenelm to do the same. "Now, young sir," said the former, "you and I can talk at our ease. That adventure of yours yesterday may be the luckiest thing that could happen to you."

"It is sufficiently lucky if I have been of any service to your niece. But her own good sense would have been her safeguard if she had been alone, and discovered, as she would have done, that Mr. Compton had, knowingly or not, misled her to believe that he was a single man."

"Hang Mr. Compton! we have done with him.
I am a plain man, and I come to the point.   It
is you who have carried off my niece; it is with
you that she came to this hotel.   Now when Elsie
told me how well you had behaved, and that your
language and manners were those of a real gentleman, my mind was made up.   I guess pretty well
what you are; you are a gentleman's son—probably a college youth—not overburthened with
cash—had a quarrel with your governor, and he
keeps you short.   Don't interrupt me.   Well, Elsie
is a good girl and a pretty girl, and will make a
good wife, as wives go; and, hark ye, she has
£20,000.   So just confide in me—and if you
don't like your parents to know about it till the
thing's done, and they be only got to forgive and
bless you, why, you shall marry Elsie before you
can say Jack Robinson."

For the first time in his life Kenelm Chillingly
was seized with terror—terror and consternation.
His jaw dropped—his tongue was palsied.   If hair
ever stands on end, his hair did.   At last, with super-
human effort, he gasped out the word, "Marry!"

"Yes—marry. If you are a gentleman you are bound to it. You have compromised my niece —a respectable, virtuous girl, sir—an orphan, but not unprotected. I repeat, it is you who have plucked her from my very arms, and with violence and assault; eloped with her; and what would the world say if it knew? Would it believe in your prudent conduct?—conduct only to be explained by the respect you felt due to your future wife. And where will you find a better? Where will you find an uncle who will part with his ward and £20,000 without asking if you have a sixpence? and the girl has taken a fancy to you —I see it; would she have given up that player so easily if you had not stolen her heart? Would you break that heart? No, young man—you are not a villain. Shake hands on it!"

"Mr. Bovill," said Kenelm, recovering his wonted equanimity, "I am inexpressibly flattered by the honour you propose to me, and I do not deny that Miss Elsie is worthy of a much better man than myself. But I have inconceivable prejudices against the connubial state. If it be per-

mitted to a member of the Established Church
to cavil at any sentence written by St. Paul—and
I think that liberty may be permitted to a simple
layman, since eminent members of the clergy cri-
ticise the whole Bible as freely as if it were the
history of Queen Elizabeth by Mr. Froude—I
should demur at the doctrine that it is better to
marry than to burn; I myself should prefer burn-
ing.   With these sentiments it would ill become
any one entitled to that distinction of 'gentleman'
which you confer on me to lead a fellow-victim
to the sacrificial altar.   As for any reproach
attached to Miss Elsie, since in my telegram I
directed you to ask for a young gentleman at this
hotel, her very sex is not known in this place unless you divulge it. And——"   .

Here Kenelm was interrupted by a violent ex-
plosion of rage from the uncle. He stamped his
feet; he almost foamed at the mouth; he doubled
his fist, and shook it in Kenelm's face.

"Sir, you are mocking me: John Bovill is not
a man to be jeered in this way. You *shall* marry
the girl.   I'll not have her thrust back upon me
to be the plague of my life with her whims and

tantrums. You have taken her, and you shall keep her, or I'll break every bone in your skin."

"Break them," said Kenelm, resignedly, but at the same time falling back into a formidable attitude of defence, which cooled the pugnacity of his accuser. Mr. Bovill sank into his chair, and wiped his forehead. Kenelm craftily pursued the advantage he had gained, and in mild accents proceeded to reason—

"When you recover your habitual serenity of humour, Mr. Bovill, you will see how much your very excusable desire to secure your niece's happiness, and, I may add, to reward what you allow to have been forbearing and well-bred conduct on my part, has hurried you into an error of judgment. You know nothing of me. I may be, for what you know, an impostor or swindler; I may have every bad quality, and yet you are to be contented with my assurance, or rather your own assumption, that I am born a gentleman, in order to give me your niece and her £20,000. This is temporary insanity on your part. Allow me to leave you to recover from your excitement."

13*

"Stop, sir," said Mr. Bovill, in a changed and
sullen tone; "I am not quite the madman you
think me. But I daresay I have been too hasty
and too rough. Nevertheless the facts are as I
have stated them, and I do not see how, as a
man of honour, you can get off marrying my
niece. The mistake you made in running away
with her was, no doubt, innocent on your part;
but still there it is; and supposing the case came
before a jury, it would be an ugly one for you
and your family. Marriage alone could mend it.
Come, come, I own I was too business-like in
rushing to the point at once, and I no longer
say, 'Marry my niece off-hand.' You have only
seen her disguised and in a false position. Pay
me a visit at Oakdale—stay with me a month—
and if, at the end of that time, you do not like
her well enough to propose, I'll let you off and
say no more about it."

While Mr. Bovill thus spoke, and Kenelm
listened, neither saw that the door had been
noiselessly opened, and that Elsie stood at the
threshold. Now, before Kenelm could reply, she

advanced into the middle of the room, and, her small figure drawn up to its fullest height, her cheeks glowing, her lips quivering, exclaimed—

"Uncle, for shame!" Then, addressing Kenelm in a sharp tone of anguish, "Oh, do not believe I knew anything of this!" she covered her face with both hands, and stood mute.

All of chivalry that Kenelm had received with his baptismal appellation was aroused. He sprang up, and, bending his knee as he drew one of her hands into his own, he said—

"I am as convinced that your uncle's words are abhorrent to you as I am that you are a pure-hearted and high-spirited woman, of whose friendship I shall be proud. We meet again." Then releasing her hand, he addressed Mr. Bovill: "Sir, you are unworthy the charge of your niece. Had you not been so, she would have committed no imprudence. If she have any female relation, to that relation transfer your charge."

"I have! I have!" cried Elsie; "my lost mother's sister—let me go to her."

"The woman who keeps a school!" said Mr. Bovill, sneeringly.

"Why not?" asked Kenelm.

"She never would go there. I proposed it to her a year ago. The minx would not go into a school."

"I will now, uncle."

"Well, then, you shall at once; and I hope you'll be put on bread and water. Fool! fool! you have spoilt your own game. Mr. Chillingly, now that Miss Elsie has turned her back on herself, I can convince you that I am not the madman you thought me. I was at the festive meeting held when you came of age—my brother is one of your father's tenants. I did not recognise your face immediately in the excitement of our encounter and in your change of dress; but in walking home it struck me that I had seen it before, and I knew it at once when you entered the room to-day. It has been a tussle between us which should beat the other. You have beat me; and thanks to that idiot! If she had not put her spoke into my wheel, she should have lived to be 'my lady.' Now good-day, sir."

"Mr. Bovill, you offered to shake hands: shake

hands now, and promise me, with the good faith of one honourable combatant to another, that Miss Elsie shall go to her aunt the schoolmistress at once if she wishes it. Hark ye, my friend" (this in Mr. Bovill's ear): "A man can never manage a woman. Till a woman marries, a prudent man leaves her to women; when she does marry, she manages her husband, and there's an end of it."

Kenelm was gone.

"Oh, wise young man!" murmured the uncle. "Elsie, dear, how can we go to your aunt's while you are in that dress?"

Elsie started as from a trance, her eyes directed towards the doorway through which Kenelm had vanished. "This dress," she said, contemptuously—"this dress—is not that easily altered with shops in the town?"

"Gad!" muttered Mr. Bovill, "that youngster is a second Solomon; and if I can't manage Elsie, she'll manage a husband—whenever she gets one."

CHAPTER VIII.

"BY the powers that guard innocence and celibacy," soliloquised Kenelm Chillingly, "but I have had a narrow escape! and had that amphibious creature been in girl's clothes instead of boy's, when she intervened like the deity of the ancient drama, I might have plunged my armorial Fishes into hot water. Though, indeed, it is hard to suppose that a young lady head-over-ears in love with Mr. Compton yesterday could have consigned her affections to me to-day. Still she looked as if she could, which proves either that one is never to trust a woman's heart, or never to trust a woman's looks. Decimus Roach is right. Man must never relax his flight from the women, if he strives to achieve an 'Approach to the Angels.' "

These reflections were made by Kenelm Chillingly as, having turned his back upon the town in which such temptations and trials had befallen him, he took his solitary way along a footpath that wound through meads and corn-fields, and shortened by three miles the distance to a cathedral town at which he proposed to rest for the night.

He had travelled for some hours, and the sun was beginning to slope towards a range of blue hills in the west, when he came to the margin of a fresh rivulet, overshadowed by feathery willows, and the quivering leaves of silvery Italian poplars. Tempted by the quiet and cool of this pleasant spot, he flung himself down on the banks, drew from his knapsack some crusts of bread with which he had wisely provided himself, and, dipping them into the pure lymph as it rippled over its pebbly bed, enjoyed one of those luxurious repasts for which epicures would exchange their banquets in return for the appetite of youth. Then, reclined along the bank, and crushing the wild thyme which grows best and sweetest in wooded coverts, provided they be neighboured by water, no matter whether in pool or rill, he resigned himself to that intermediate state be-

tween thought and dreamland which we call
'reverie.'   At a little distance he heard the low
still sound of the mower's scythe, and the air
came to his brow sweet with the fragrance of new-
mown hay.

He was roused by a gentle tap on the shoulder,
and turning lazily round, saw a good-humoured
jovial face upon a pair of massive shoulders, and
heard a hearty and winning voice say—

"Young man, if you are not too tired, will
you lend a hand to get in my hay? We are very
short of hands, and I am afraid we shall have
rain pretty soon."

Kenelm rose and shook himself, gravely ·con-
templated the stranger, and replied, in his customary sententious fashion, "Man is born to help
his fellow-man—especially to get in hay while the
sun shines.   I am at your service."

"That's a good fellow, and I'm greatly obliged
to you.   You see I had counted on a gang of
roving haymakers, but they were bought up by
another farmer.   This way,"—and leading on
through a gap in the brushwood, he emerged,

followed by Kenelm, into a large meadow, one-
third of which was still under the scythe, the
rest being occupied with persons of both sexes,
tossing and spreading the cut grass. Among the
latter, Kenelm, stripped to his shirt-sleeves, soon
found himself tossing and spreading like the rest,
with his usual melancholy resignation of mien
and aspect. Though a little awkward at first in
the use of his unfamiliar implements, his practice
in all athletic accomplishments bestowed on him
that invaluable quality which is termed 'handi-
ness,' and he soon distinguished himself by the
superior activity and neatness with which he
performed his work. Something—it might be in
his countenance or in the charm of his being a
stranger—attracted the attention of the feminine
section of haymakers, and one very pretty girl
who was nearer to him than the rest, attempted
to commence conversation.

"This is new to you," she said, smiling.

"Nothing is new to me," answered Kenelm,
mournfully. "But allow me to observe, that to
do things well you should only do one thing at

a time. I am here to make hay, and not conversation."

"My!" said the girl, in amazed ejaculation,
and turned off with a toss of her pretty head.

"I wonder if that jade has got an uncle,"
thought Kenelm.

The farmer, who took his share of work with
the men, halting now and then to look round,
noticed Kenelm's vigorous application with much
approval, and at the close of the day's work
shook him heartily by the hand, leaving a two-
shilling piece in his palm. The heir of the
Chillinglys gazed on that honorarium, and turned
it over with the finger and thumb of the left hand.

"Ben't it eno'?" said the farmer, nettled.

"Pardon me," answered Kenelm. "But, to
tell you the truth, it is the first money I ever
earned by my own bodily labour; and I regard
it with equal curiosity and respect. But, if it
would not offend you, I would rather that, instead
of the money, you had offered me some supper;
for I have tasted nothing but bread and water
since the morning."

"You shall have the money and supper both, my lad," said the farmer, cheerily. "And if you will stay and help till I have got in the hay, I daresay my good woman can find you a better bed than you'll get at the village inn—if, indeed, you can get one there at all."

"You are very kind. But before I accept your hospitality excuse one question—have you any nieces about you?"

"Nieces!" echoed the farmer, mechanically thrusting his hands into his breeches-pockets, as if in search of something there—"nieces about me! what do you mean? Be that a newfangled word for coppers?"

"Not for coppers, though perhaps for brass. But I spoke without metaphor. I object to nieces upon abstract principle, confirmed by the test of experience."

The farmer stared, and thought his new friend not quite so sound in his mental as he evidently was in his physical conformation, but replied, with a laugh, "Make yourself easy, then. I have only one niece, and she is married to an iron-monger and lives in Exeter."

On entering the farmhouse, Kenelm's host conducted him straight into the kitchen, and cried out, in a hearty voice, to a comely middle-aged dame, who, with a stout girl, was intent on culinary operations, "Holloa! old woman, I have brought you a guest who has well earned his supper, for he has done the work of two, and I have promised him a bed."

The farmer's wife turned sharply round. "He is heartily welcome to supper. As to a bed," she said, doubtfully, "I don't know." But here her eyes settled on Kenelm; and there was some-thing in his aspect so unlike what she expected to see in an itinerant haymaker, that she in-voluntarily dropped a curtsy, and resumed, with a change of tone, "The gentleman shall have the guest-room; but it will take a little time to get ready—you know, John, all the furniture is covered up."

"Well, wife, there will be leisure eno' for that. He don't want to go to roost till he has supped."

"Certainly not," said Kenelm, sniffing a very agreeable odour.

"Where are the girls?" asked the farmer.

"They have been in these five minutes, and gone up-stairs to tidy themselves."

"What girls?" faltered Kenelm, retreating towards the door. "I thought you said you had no nieces."

"But I did not say I had no daughters. Why, you are not afraid of them, are you?"

"Sir," replied Kenelm, with a polite and politic evasion of that question, "if your daughters are like their mother, you can't say that they are not dangerous."

"Come," cried the farmer, looking very much pleased, while his dame smiled and blushed— "come, that's as nicely said as if you were canvassing the county. 'Tis not among haymakers that you learned manners, I guess; and perhaps I have been making too free with my betters."

"What!" quoth the courteous Kenelm, "do you mean to imply that you were too free with your shillings? Apologise for that, if you like,

but I don't think you'll get back the shillings. I
have not seen so much of this life as you have,
but, according to my experience, when a man
once parts with his money, whether to his betters
or his worsers, the chances are that he'll never
see it again."

At this aphorism the farmer laughed ready
to kill himself, his wife chuckled, and even the
maid-of-all-work grinned.   Kenelm, preserving
his unalterable gravity, said to himself—

"Wit consists in the epigrammatic expression
of a commonplace truth, and the dullest remark
on the worth of money is almost as sure of
successful appreciation as the dullest remark on
the worthlessness of women. Certainly I am a
wit without knowing it."

Here the farmer touched him on the shoulder
—touched it, did not slap it, as he would have
done ten minutes before—and said—

"We must not disturb the Missis or we shall
get no supper. I'll just go and give a look into
the cowsheds. Do you know much about cows?"

"Yes, cows produce cream and butter. The

best cows are those which produce at the least cost the best cream and butter. But how the best cream and butter can be produced at a price which will place them free of expense on a poor man's breakfast-table, is a question to be settled by a Reformed Parliament and a Liberal Administration. In the meanwhile let us not delay the supper."

The farmer and his guest quitted the kitchen and entered the farmyard.

"You are quite a stranger in these parts?"

"Quite."

"You don't even know my name?"

"No, except that I heard your wife call you John."

"My name is John Saunderson."

"Ah! you come from the north, then? That's why you are so sensible and shrewd. Names that end in 'son' are chiefly borne by the descendants of the Danes, to whom King Alfred, heaven bless him, peacefully assigned no less than sixteen English counties. And when a Dane was called somebody's son, it is a sign that he was the son of a somebody."

"By gosh! I never heard that before."

"If I thought you had I should not have said it."

"Now I have told you my name, what is yours?"

"A wise man asks questions and a fool answers them. Suppose for a moment that I am not a fool."

Farmer Saunderson scratched his head, and looked more puzzled than became the descendant of a Dane settled by King Alfred in the north of England.

"Dash it," said he at last, "but I think you are Yorkshire too."

"Man, who is the most conceited of all animals, says that he alone has the prerogative of thought, and condemns the other animals to the meaner mechanical operation which he calls instinct. But as instincts are unerring and thoughts generally go wrong, man has not much to boast of according to his own definition. When you say you think, and take it for granted, that I am Yorkshire, you err. I am not Yorkshire. Confining yourself to instinct, can you divine when we shall sup? The cows you are about to visit divine to a moment when they shall be fed."

Said the farmer, recovering his sense of superiority to the guest whom he obliged with a supper, "In ten minutes." Then, after a pause, and in a tone of deprecation, as if he feared he might be thought fine, he continued—"We don't sup in the kitchen. My father did, and so did I till I married; but my Bess, though she's as good a farmer's wife as ever wore shoe-leather, was a tradesman's daughter, and had been brought up different. You see, she was not without a good bit of money; but even if she had been, I should not have liked her folks to say I had lowered her —so we sup in the parlour."

Quoth Kenelm, "The first consideration is to sup at all. Supper conceded, every man is more likely to get on in life who would rather sup in his parlour than his kitchen. Meanwhile, I see a pump; while you go to the cows I will stay here and wash my hands of them."

"Hold; you seem a sharp fellow, and cer-

14*

tainly no fool. I have a son, a good smart chap, but stuck up; crows it over us all; thinks no small beer of himself. You'd do me a service, and him too, if you'd let him down a peg or two."

Kenelm, who was now hard at work at the pump-handle, only replied by a gracious nod. But as he seldom lost an opportunity for re-flection, he said to himself, while he laved his face in the stream from the spout, "One can't wonder why every small man thinks it so pleasant to let down a big one, when a father asks a stranger to let down his own son for even fancying that he is not small beer. It is upon that principle in human nature that criticism wisely relinquishes its pretensions as an analytical science, and becomes a lucrative profession. It relies on the pleasure its readers find in letting a man down."

CHAPTER IX.

IT was a pretty, quaint farmhouse, such as might go well with two or three hundred acres of tolerably good land, tolerably well farmed by an active old-fashioned tenant, who, though he did not use mowing-machines nor steam-ploughs, nor dabble in chemical experiments, still brought an adequate capital to his land, and made the capital yield a very fair return of interest. The supper was laid out in a good-sized though low-pitched parlour with a glazed door, now wide open, as were all the latticed windows, looking into a small garden, rich in those straggling old English flowers which are nowadays banished from gardens more pretentious and infinitely less fragrant. At one corner was an arbour covered with honeysuckle, and, opposite to it, a row of beehives. The room itself had an air of comfort, and that sort of elegance which indicates the pre-

siding genius of feminine taste. There were
shelves suspended to the wall by blue ribbons,
and filled with small books neatly bound; there
were flower-pots in all the window-sills; there
was a small cottage piano; the walls were graced
partly with engraved portraits of county magnates
and prize oxen, partly with samplers in worsted-
work, comprising verses of moral character and
the names and birthdays of the farmer's grand-
mother, mother, wife, and daughters. Over the
chimney-piece was a small mirror, and above that
the trophy of a fox's brush; while niched into an
angle in the room was a glazed cupboard, rich
with specimens of old china, Indian and English.

The party consisted of the farmer, his wife,
three buxom daughters, and a pale-faced slender
lad of about twenty, the only son, who did not
take willingly to farming: he had been educated
at a superior grammar school, and had high notions about the March of Intellect and the Progress of the Age.

Kenelm, though among the gravest of mortals, was one of the least shy. In fact shyness is

the usual symptom of a keen *amour propre;* and of that quality the youthful Chillingly scarcely possessed more than did the three Fishes of his hereditary scutcheon. He felt himself perfectly at home with his entertainers; taking care, however, that his attentions were so equally divided between the three daughters as to prevent all suspicion of a particular preference. "There is safety in numbers," thought he, "especially in odd numbers. The three Graces never married, neither did the nine Muses."

"I presume, young ladies, that you are fond of music," said Kenelm, glancing at the piano.

"Yes, I love it dearly," said the eldest girl, speaking for the others.

Quoth the farmer, as he heaped the stranger's plate with boiled beef and carrots, "Things are not what they were when I was a boy; then it was only great tenant-farmers who had their girls taught the piano, and sent their boys to a good school. Now we small folks are for helping our children a step or two higher than our own place on the ladder."

"The schoolmaster is abroad," said the son, with the emphasis of a sage adding an original aphorism to the stores of philosophy.

"There is, no doubt, a greater equality of culture than there was in the last generation," said Kenelm. "People of all ranks utter the same commonplace ideas in very much the same arrangements of syntax. And in proportion as the democracy of intelligence extends—a friend of mine, who is a doctor, tells me that complaints formerly reserved to what is called the aristocracy (though what that word means in plain English I don't know) are equally shared by the commonalty—*tic-douloureux* and other neuralgic maladies abound. And the human race, in England at least, is becoming more slight and delicate. There is a fable of a man who, when he became exceedingly old, was turned into a grasshopper. England is very old, and is evidently approaching the grasshopper state of development. Perhaps we don't eat as much beef as our forefathers did. May I ask you for another slice?"

Kenelm's remarks were somewhat over the

heads of his audience. But the son, taking them as a slur upon the enlightened spirit of the age, coloured up and said, with a knitted brow, "I hope, sir, that you are not an enemy to progress."

"That depends: for instance, I prefer staying here, where I am well off, to going farther and faring worse."

"Well said!" cried the farmer.

Not deigning to notice that interruption, the son took up Kenelm's reply with a sneer, "I suppose you mean that it is to fare worse, if you march with the time."

"I am afraid we have no option but to march with the time; but when we reach that stage when to march any farther is to march into old age, we should not be sorry if time would be kind enough to stand still; and all good doctors concur in advising us to do nothing to hurry him."

"There is no sign of old age in this country, sir; and thank heaven we are not standing still!"

"Grasshoppers never do; they are always hopping and jumping, and making what they think 'progress,' till (unless they hop into the water and are swallowed up prematurely by a carp or a frog) they die of the exhaustion which hops and jumps unremitting naturally produce. May I ask you, Mrs. Saunderson, for some of that rice-pudding?"

The farmer, who, though he did not quite comprehend Kenelm's metaphorical mode of arguing, saw delightedly that his wise son looked more posed than himself, cried with great glee, "Bob, my boy,—Bob! our visitor is a little too much for you!"

"Oh no," said Kenelm, modestly. "But I honestly think Mr. Bob would be a wiser man, and a weightier man, and more removed from the grasshopper state, if he would think less and eat more pudding."

When the supper was over the farmer offered Kenelm a clay pipe filled with shag, which that adventurer accepted with his habitual resignation to the ills of life; and the whole party, excepting

Mrs. Saunderson, strolled into the garden. Kenelm and Mr. Saunderson seated themselves in the honeysuckle arbour: the girls and the advocate of progress stood without among the garden flowers. It was a still and lovely night, the moon at her full. The farmer, seated facing his hay-fields, smoked on placidly. Kenelm, at the third whiff, laid aside his pipe, and glanced furtively at the three Graces. They formed a pretty group, all clustered together near the silenced beehives, the two younger seated on the grass strip that bordered the flower-beds, their arms over each other's shoulders, the elder one standing behind them, with the moonlight shining soft on her auburn hair.

Young Saunderson walked restlessly by himself to and fro the path of gravel.

"It is a strange thing," ruminated Kenelm, "that girls are not unpleasant to look at if you take them collectively—two or three bound up together; but if you detach any one of them from the bunch, the odds are that she is as plain as a pikestaff. I wonder whether that bucolical

grasshopper, who is so enamoured of the hop
and jump that he calls 'progress,' classes the
society of the Mormons among the evidences of
civilised advancement.   There is a good deal to
be said in favour of taking a whole lot of wives
as one may buy a whole lot of cheap razors. For
it is not impossible that out of a dozen a good
one may be found.   And then, too, a whole
nosegay of variegated blooms, with a faded leaf
here and there, must be more agreeable to the
eye than the same monotonous solitary lady's
smock.   But I fear these reflections are naughty;
let us change them.   Farmer," he said aloud, "I
suppose your handsome daughters are too fine
to assist you much. I did not see them among
the haymakers."

"Oh, they were there, but by themselves, in
the back part of the field.   I did not want them
to mix with all the girls, many of whom are
strangers from other places. I don't know anything
against them; but as I don't know anything for
them, I thought it as well to keep my lasses apart."

"But I should have supposed it wiser to keep

your son apart from them. I saw him in the thick of those nymphs."

"Well," said the farmer, musingly, and withdrawing his pipe from his lips, "I don't think lasses not quite well brought up, poor things! do as much harm to the lads as they can do to proper-behaved lasses—leastways my wife does not think so. 'Keep good girls from bad girls,' says she, 'and good girls will never go wrong.' And you will find there is something in that when you have girls of your own to take care of."

"Without waiting for that time—which I trust may never occur—I can recognise the wisdom of your excellent wife's observation. My own opinion is, that a woman can more easily do mischief to her own sex than to ours,—since, of course, she cannot exist without doing mischief to somebody or other."

"And good, too," said the jovial farmer, thumping his fist on the table. "What should we be without the women?"

"Very much better, I take it, sir. Adam was

as good as gold, and never had a qualm of conscience or stomach till Eve seduced him into
eating raw apples."

"Young man, thou'st been crossed in love.
I see it now. That's why thou look'st so sorrowful."

"Sorrowful! Did you ever know a man
crossed in love who looked less sorrowful when
he came across a pudding?"

"Hey! but thou canst ply a good knife and
fork—that I will say for thee." Here the farmer
turned round, and gazed on Kenelm with deliberate scrutiny. That scrutiny accomplished, his
voice took a somewhat more respectful tone, as
he resumed, "Do you know that you puzzle me
somewhat?"

"Very likely. I am sure that I puzzle myself.
Say on."

"Looking at your dress and—and——"

"The two shillings you gave me? Yes——"

"I took you for the son of some small farmer
like myself. But now I judge from your talk that

you are a college chap—anyhow a gentleman.
Ben't it so?"

"My dear Mr. Saunderson, I set out on my
travels, which is not long ago, with a strong
dislike to telling lies. But I doubt if a man can
get long through this world without finding that
the faculty of lying was bestowed on him by
nature as a necessary means of self-preservation.
If you are going to ask me any questions about
myself, I am sure that I shall tell you lies. Perhaps, therefore, it may be best for both if I
decline the bed you proffered me, and take my
night's rest under a hedge."

"Pooh! I don't want to know more of a man's
affairs than he thinks fit to tell me. Stay and
finish the haymaking. And I say, lad, I'm glad
you don't seem to care for the girls; for I saw a
very pretty one trying to flirt with you—and if
you don't mind she'll bring you into trouble."

"How? Does she want to run away from her
uncle?"

"Uncle! Bless you, she don't live with him!
She lives with her father; and I never knew that

she wants to run away. In fact, Jessie Wiles—
that's her name—is, I believe, a very good girl,
and everybody likes her—perhaps a little too
much; but then she knows she's a beauty, and
does not object to admiration."

"No woman ever does, whether she's a beauty
or not. But I don't yet understand why Jessie
Wiles should bring me into trouble."

"Because there is a big hulking fellow who
has gone half out of his wits for her; and when
he fancies he sees any other chap too sweet on
her he thrashes him into a jelly. So, youngster,
you just keep your skin out of that trap."

"Hem! And what does the girl say to those
proofs of affection? Does she like the man the
better for thrashing other admirers into jelly?"

"Poor child! No; she hates the very sight of
him. But he swears she shall marry nobody else,
if he hangs for it. And to tell you the truth, I
suspect that if Jessie does seem to trifle with
others a little too lightly, it is to draw away this
bully's suspicion from the only man I think she
does care for—a poor sickly young fellow who

was crippled by an accident, and whom Tom Bowles could brain with his little finger."

"This is really interesting," cried Kenelm, showing something like excitement. "I should like to know this terrible suitor."

"That's easy eno'," said the farmer, dryly. "You have only to take a stroll with Jessie Wiles after sunset, and you'll know more of Tom Bowles than you are likely to forget in a month."

"Thank you very much for your information," said Kenelm, in a soft tone, grateful but pensive. "I hope to profit by it."

"Do. I should be sorry if any harm came to thee; and Tom Bowles in one of his furies is as bad to cross as a mad bull. So now, as we must be up early, I'll just take a look round the stables, and then off to bed; and I advise you to do the same."

"Thank you for the hint. I see the young ladies have already gone in. Good-night."

Passing through the garden, Kenelm encountered the junior Saunderson.

"I fear," said the Votary of Progress, "that

you have found the governor awful slow. What have you been talking about?"

"Girls," said Kenelm, "a subject always awful, but not necessarily slow."

"Girls—the governor been talking about girls! You joke."

"I wish I did joke, but that is a thing I could never do since I came upon earth. Even in the cradle, I felt that life was a very serious matter, and did not allow of jokes. I remember too well my first dose of castor-oil. You too, Mr. Bob, have doubtless imbibed that initiatory preparation to the sweets of existence. The corners of your mouth have not recovered from the downward curves into which it so rigidly dragged them. Like myself, you are of grave temperament, and not easily moved to jocularity—nay, an enthusiast for Progress is of necessity a man eminently dissatisfied with the present state of affairs. And chronic dissatisfaction resents the momentary relief of a joke."

"Give off chaffing, if you please," said Bob, lowering the didascular intonations of his voice, "and just tell me plainly, did not my father say anything particular about me?"

"Not a word—the only person of the male sex of whom he said anything particular was Tom Bowles."

"What, fighting Tom! the terror of the whole neighbourhood! Ah, I guess the old gentleman is afraid lest Tom may fall foul upon me. But Jessie Wiles is not worth a quarrel with that brute. It is a crying shame in the Government——"

"What! has the Government failed to appreciate the heroism of Tom Bowles, or rather to restrain the excesses of its ardour?"

"Stuff! it is a shame in the Government not to have compelled his father to put him to school. If education were universal——"

"You think there would be no brutes in particular. It may be so, but education is universal in China. And so is the bastinado. I thought, however, that you said the schoolmaster was abroad, and that the age of enlightenment was in full progress."

"Yes, in the towns, but not in these obsolete

15*

rural districts; and that brings me to the point.
I feel lost—thrown away here. I have something
in me, sir, and it can only come out by collision
with equal minds. So do me a favour, will
you?"

"With the greatest pleasure."

"Give the governor a hint that he can't expect me, after the education I have had, to follow
the plough and fatten pigs; and that Manchester
is the place for ME."

"Why Manchester?"

"Because I have a relation in business there
who will give me a clerkship if the governor will
consent. And Manchester rules England."

"Mr. Bob Saunderson, I will do my best to
promote your wishes. This is a land of liberty,
and every man should choose his own walk in it,
so that, at the last, if he goes to the dogs, he
goes to them without that disturbance of temper
which is naturally occasioned by the sense of
being driven to their jaws by another man against
his own will. He has then no one to blame but
himself. And that, Mr. Bob, is a great comfort.

When, having got into a scrape, we blame others, we unconsciously become unjust, spiteful, uncharitable, malignant, perhaps revengeful. We indulge in feelings which tend to demoralise the whole character. But when we only blame ourselves, we become modest and penitent. We make allowances for others. And, indeed, self-blame is a salutary exercise of conscience, which a really good man performs every day of his life. And now, will you show me the room in which I am to sleep, and forget for a few hours that I am alive at all—the best thing that can happen to us in this world, my dear Mr. Bob! There's never much amiss with our days, so long as we can forget all about them the moment we lay our heads on the pillow."

The two young men entered the house amicably, arm in arm. The girls had already retired, but Mrs. Saunderson was still up to conduct her visitor to the guest's chamber—a pretty room which had been furnished twenty-two years ago, on the occasion of the farmer's marriage, at the expense of Mrs. Saunderson's mother, for her own occupation whenever she paid them a visit. And with its dimity curtains and trellised paper it still looked as fresh and new as if decorated and furnished yesterday.

Left alone, Kenelm undressed, and before he got into bed, bared his right arm, and doubling it, gravely contemplated its muscular development, passing his left hand over that prominence in the upper part which is vulgarly called the ball. Satisfied apparently with the size and the firmness of that pugilistic protuberance, he gently sighed forth, "I fear I shall have to lick Thomas Bowles." In five minutes more he was asleep.

CHAPTER X.

THE next day the hay-mowing was completed, and a large portion of the hay already made carted away to be stacked. Kenelm acquitted himself with a credit not less praiseworthy than had previously won Mr. Saunderson's approbation. But instead of rejecting as before the acquaintance of Miss Jessie Wiles, he contrived towards noon to place himself near to that dangerous beauty, and commenced conversation. "I am afraid I was rather rude to you yesterday, and I want to beg pardon."

"Oh," answered the girl, in that simple intelligible English which is more frequent among our village folks nowadays than many popular novelists would lead us into supposing—"oh, I ought to ask pardon for taking a liberty in speaking to you. But I thought you'd feel strange, and I intended it kindly."

"I'm sure you did," returned Kenelm, chivalrously raking her portion of hay as well as his own, while he spoke. "And I want to be good friends with you. It is very near the time when we shall leave off for dinner, and Mrs. Saunderson has filled my pockets with some excellent beef-sandwiches, which I shall be happy to share with you, if you do not object to dine with me here, instead of going home for your dinner."

The girl hesitated, and then shook her head in dissent from the proposition.

"Are you afraid that your neighbours will think it wrong?"

Jessie curled up her lip with a pretty scorn, and said, "I don't much care what other folks say, but isn't it wrong?"

"Not in the least. Let me make your mind easy. I am here but for a day or two; we are not likely ever to meet again; but, before I go, I should be glad if I could do you some little service." As he spoke he had paused from his work, and, leaning on his rake, fixed his eyes for the first time attentively, on the fair hay-maker.

Yes, she was decidedly pretty—pretty to a rare degree—luxuriant brown hair neatly tied up, under a straw hat doubtless of her own plaiting; for, as a general rule, nothing more educates the village maid for the destinies of flirt, than the accomplishment of straw-plaiting. She had large, soft blue eyes, delicate small features, and a complexion more clear in its healthful bloom than rural beauties generally retain against the influences of wind and sun. She smiled and slightly coloured as he gazed on her, and, lifting her eyes, gave him one gentle, trustful glance, which might have bewitched a philosopher and deceived a *roué*. And yet Kenelm, by that intuitive knowledge of character which is often truthfulest where it is least disturbed by the doubts and cavils of acquired knowledge, felt at once that in that girl's mind coquetry, perhaps unconscious, was conjoined with an innocence of anything worse than coquetry as complete as a child's. He bowed his head, in withdrawing his gaze, and took her into his heart as tenderly as if she had been a child appealing to it for protection.

"Certainly," he said inly—"certainly I must lick Tom Bowles; yet stay, perhaps after all she likes him."

"But," he continued aloud, "you do not see how I can be of any service to you. Before I explain, let me ask which of the men in the field is Tom Bowles?"

"Tom Bowles!" exclaimed Jessie, in a tone of surprise and alarm, and turning pale as she looked hastily round; "you frightened me, sir, but he is not here; he does not work in the fields. But how came you to hear of Tom Bowles?"

"Dine with me and I'll tell you. Look, there is a quiet place in yon corner under the thorn-trees by that piece of water. See, they are leaving off work: I will go for a can of beer, and then, pray, let me join you there."

Jessie paused for a moment as if doubtful still; then again glancing at Kenelm, and assured by the grave kindness of his countenance, uttered a scarce audible assent, and moved away towards the thorn-trees.

As the sun now stood perpendicularly over their heads, and the hand of the clock in the village church tower, soaring over the hedgerows, reached the first hour after noon, all work ceased in a sudden silence; some of the girls went back to their homes; those who stayed grouped together, apart from the men, who took their way to the shadows of a large oak-tree in the hedgerow, where beer kegs and cans awaited them.

CHAPTER XI.

"AND now," said Kenelm, as the two young persons, having finished their simple repast, sat under the thorn-trees and by the side of the water, fringed at that part with tall reeds through which the light summer breeze stirred with a pleasant murmur,—"now I will talk to you about Tom Bowles. Is it true that you don't like that brave young fellow?—I say young, as I take his youth for granted."

"Like him! I hate the sight of him."

"Did you always hate the sight of him? You must surely at one time have allowed him to think that you did not?"

The girl winced, and made no answer, but plucked a daffodil from the soil, and tore it ruthlessly to pieces.

"I am afraid you like to serve your admirers as you do that ill-fated flower," said Kenelm, with some severity of tone. "But concealed in the flower you may sometimes find the sting of a bee. I see by your countenance that you did not tell Tom Bowles that you hated him till it was too late to prevent his losing his wits for you."

"No; I wasn't so bad as that," said Jessie, looking, nevertheless, rather ashamed of herself; "but I was silly and giddy-like, I own; and, when he first took notice of me, I was pleased, without thinking much of it, because, you see, Mr. Bowles (emphasis on *Mr.*) is higher up than a poor girl like me. He is a tradesman, and I am only a shepherd's daughter—though, indeed, father is more like Mr. Saunderson's foreman than a mere shepherd. But I never thought anything serious of it, and did not suppose he did—that is, at first."

"So Tom Bowles is a tradesman. What trade?"

"A farrier, sir."

"And, I am told, a very fine young man."

"I don't know as to that: he is very big."

"And what made you hate him?"

"The first thing that made me hate him was,

that he insulted father, who is a very quiet, timid man, and threatened, I don't know what, if father did not make me keep company with him. Make me indeed! But Mr. Bowles is a dangerous, bad-hearted, violent man, and—don't laugh at me, sir—but I dreamed one night he was murdering me. And I think he will too, if he stays here; and so does his poor mother, who is a very nice woman, and wants him to go away; but he'll not."

"Jessie," said Kenelm, softly, "I said I wanted to make friends with you. Do you think you can make a friend of me? I can never be more than friend. But I should like to be that. Can you trust me as one?"

"Yes," answered the girl firmly, and, as she lifted her eyes to him, their look was pure from all vestige of coquetry—guileless, frank, grateful.

"Is there not another young man who courts you more civilly than Tom Bowles does, and whom you really could find it in your heart to like?"

Jessie looked round for another daffodil, and, not finding one, contented herself with a blue-bell, which she did not tear to pieces, but caressed with a tender hand. Kenelm bent his eyes down on her charming face with something in their gaze rarely seen there—something of that unreasoning, inexpressible human fondness, for which philosophers of his school have no excuse. Had ordinary mortals, like you or myself, for instance, peered through the leaves of the thorn-trees, we should have sighed or frowned, according to our several temperaments; but we should all have said, whether spitefully or envyingly, "Happy young lovers!" and should all have blundered lamentably in so saying.

Still, there is no denying the fact that a pretty face has a very unfair advantage over a plain one. And, much to the discredit of Kenelm's philanthropy, it may be reasonably doubted whether, had Jessie Wiles been endowed by nature with a snub nose and a squint, Kenelm would have volunteered his friendly services, or meditated battle with Tom Bowles on her behalf.

But there was no touch of envy or jealousy in the tone with which he said—

"I see there is some one you would like well

enough to marry, and that you make a great difference in the way you treat a daffodil and a
blue-bell. Who and what is the young man
whom the blue-bell represents? Come, confide."

"We were much brought up together," said
Jessie, still looking down, and still smoothing the
leaves of the blue-bell. "His mother lived in
the next cottage; and my mother was very fond
of him, and so was father too; and, before I was
ten years old, they used to laugh when poor Will
called me his little wife." Here the tears which
had started to Jessie's eyes began to fall over
the flower. "But now father would not hear of
it; and it can't be. And I've tried to care for
some one else, and I can't, and that's the truth."

"But why? Has he turned out ill?—taken to
poaching or drink?"

"No—no—no,—he's as steady and good a
lad as ever lived. But—but——"

"Yes; but——"

"He is a cripple now—and I love him all the
better for it." Here Jessie fairly sobbed.

Kenelm was greatly moved, and prudently
held his peace till she had a little recovered her-

self; then, in answer to his gentle questionings, he learned that Will Somers—till then a healthy and strong lad—had fallen from the height of a scaffolding, at the age of sixteen, and been so seriously injured that he was moved at once to the hospital. When he came out of it—what with the fall, and what with the long illness which had followed the effects of the accident—he was not only crippled for life, but of health so delicate and weakly that he was no longer fit for outdoor labour and the hard life of a peasant. He was an only son of a widowed mother, and his sole mode of assisting her was a very precarious one. He had taught himself basket-making; and though, Jessie said, his work was very ingenious and clever, still there were but few customers for it in that neighbourhood. And, alas! even if Jessie's father would consent to give his daughter to the poor cripple, how could the poor cripple earn enough to maintain a wife?

"And," said Jessie, "still I was happy, walking out with him on Sunday evenings, or going to sit with him and his mother—for we are both young and can wait. But I daren't do it any more now —for Tom Bowles has sworn that if I do he will beat him before my eyes; and Will has a high spirit, and I should break my heart if any harm happened to him on my account."

"As for Mr. Bowles, we'll not think of him at present. But if Will could maintain himself and you, your father would not object, nor you either, to a marriage with the poor cripple?"

"Father would not; and as for me, if it weren't for disobeying father, I'd marry him to-morrow. *I* can work."

"They are going back to the hay now; but after that task is over, let me walk home with you, and show me Will's cottage and Mr. Bowles's shop or forge."

"But you'll not say anything to Mr. Bowles. He wouldn't mind you're being a gentleman, as I now see you are, sir; and he's dangerous—oh, so dangerous!—and so strong."

"Never fear," answered Kenelm, with the nearest approach to a laugh he had ever made since childhood; "but when we are relieved, wait for me a few minutes at yon gate."

CHAPTER XII.

KENELM spoke no more to his new friend in the hay-fields; but when the day's work was over he looked round for the farmer to make an excuse for not immediately joining the family supper. However, he did not see either Mr. Saunderson or his son. Both were busied in the stackyard. Well pleased to escape excuse and the questions it might provoke, Kenelm therefore put on the coat he had laid aside and joined Jessie, who had waited for him at the gate. They entered the lane side by side, following the stream of villagers who were slowly wending their homeward way. It was a primitive English village, not adorned on the one hand with fancy or model cottages, nor on the other hand indicating penury and squalor. The church rose before them grey and Gothic, backed by the red clouds in which the sun had set, and bordered by the glebe-land of the half-seen parsonage. Then

16*

came the village green, with a pretty schoolhouse; and to this succeeded a long street of scattered whitewashed cottages, in the midst of their own little gardens.

As they walked, the moon rose in full splendour, silvering the road before them.

"Who is the squire here?" asked Kenelm. "I should guess him to be a good sort of man, and well off."

"Yes, Squire Travers; he is a great gentleman, and they say very rich. But his place is a good way from this village. You can see it if you stay, for he gives a harvest-home supper on Saturday, and Mr. Saunderson and all his tenants are going. It is a beautiful park, and Miss Travers is a sight to look at. Oh, she is lovely!" continued Jessie, with an unaffected burst of admiration; for women are more sensible of the charm of each other's beauty than men give them credit for.

"As pretty as yourself?"

"Oh, pretty is not the word. She is a thousand times handsomer!"

"Humph!" said Kenelm, incredulously.

There was a pause, broken by a quick sigh from Jessie.

"What are you sighing for?—tell me."

"I was thinking that a very little can make folks happy, but that somehow or other that very little is as hard to get as if one set one's heart on a great deal."

"That's very wisely said. Everybody covets a little something for which, perhaps, nobody else would give a straw. But what's the very little thing for which you are sighing?"

"Mrs. Bawtrey wants to sell that shop of hers. She is getting old, and has had fits; and she can get nobody to buy; and if Will had that shop and I could keep it—but 'tis no use thinking of that."

"What shop do you mean?"

"There!"

"Where? I see no shop."

"But it is *the* shop of the village—the only one, where the post-office is."

"Ah! I see something at the windows like a red cloak. What do they sell?"

"Everything—tea and sugar, and candles, and shawls, and gowns, and cloaks, and mouse-traps, and letter-paper; and Mrs. Bawtrey buys poor Will's baskets, and sells them for a good deal more than she pays."

"It seems a nice cottage, with a field and orchard at the back."

"Yes. Mrs. Bawtrey pays £8 a-year for it; but the shop can well afford it."

Kenelm made no reply. They both walked on in silence, and had now reached the centre of the village street when Jessie, looking up, uttered an abrupt exclamation, gave an affrighted start, and then came to a dead stop.

Kenelm's eye followed the direction of hers, and saw, a few yards distant, at the other side of the way, a small red brick house, with thatched sheds adjoining it, the whole standing in a wide yard, over the gate of which leaned a man smoking a small cutty-pipe. "It is Tom Bowles," whispered Jessie, and instinctively she twined her arm into Kenelm's—then, as if on second thoughts, withdrew it, and said, still in a whisper, "Go back now, sir—do."

"Not I. It is Tom Bowles whom I want to know. Hush!"

For here Tom Bowles had thrown down his pipe and was coming slowly across the road towards them.

Kenelm eyed him with attention. A singularly powerful man, not so tall as Kenelm by some inches, but still above the middle height, herculean shoulders and chest, the lower limbs not in equal proportion—a sort of slouching, shambling gait. As he advanced the moonlight fell on his face,—it was a handsome one. He wore no hat, and his hair, of a light brown, curled close. His face was fresh-coloured, with aquiline features; his age apparently about six-or seven-and-twenty. Coming nearer and nearer, whatever favourable impression the first glance at his physiognomy might have made on Kenelm was dispelled, for the expression of his face changed and became fierce and lowering.

Kenelm was still walking on, Jessie by his

side, when Bowles rudely thrust himself between them, and seizing the girl's arm with one hand, he turned his face full on Kenelm, with a menacing wave of the other hand, and said in a deep burly voice—

"Who be you?"

"Let go that young woman before I tell you."

"If you weren't a stranger," answered Bowles, seeming as if he tried to suppress a rising fit of wrath, "you'd be in the kennel for those words. But I s'pose you don't know that I'm Tom Bowles, and I don't choose the girl as I'm after to keep company with any other man. So you be off."

"And I don't choose any other man to lay violent hands on any girl walking by my side without telling him that he's a brute; and that I only wait till he has both his hands at liberty to let him know that he has not a poor cripple to deal with."

Tom Bowles could scarcely believe his ears. Amaze swallowed up for the moment every other sentiment. Mechanically he loosened his hold of Jessie, who fled off like a bird released. But evidently she thought of her new friend's danger more than her own escape; for instead of sheltering herself in her father's cottage, she ran towards a group of labourers, who, near at hand, had stopped loitering before the public-house and returned with those allies towards the spot in which she had left the two men. She was very popular with the villagers, who, strong in the sense of numbers, overcame their awe of Tom Bowles, and arrived at the place half running, half striding, in time, they hoped, to interpose between his terrible arm and the bones of the unoffending stranger.

Meanwhile Bowles, having recovered his first astonishment, and scarcely noticing Jessie's escape, still left his right arm extended towards the place she had vacated, and with a quick back-stroke of the left levelled at Kenelm's face, growled contemptuously, "Thou'lt find one hand enough for thee."

But quick as was his aim, Kenelm caught the

lifted arm just above the elbow, causing the blow
to waste itself on air, and with a simultaneous
advance of his right knee and foot dexterously
tripped up his bulky antagonist, and laid him
sprawling on his back. The movement was so
sudden, and the stun it occasioned so utter, morally
as well as physically, that a minute or more
elapsed before Tom Bowles picked himself up.
And he then stood another minute glowering at
his antagonist, with a vague sentiment of awe
almost like a superstitious panic. For it is notice-
able that, however fierce and fearless a man or
even a wild beast may be, yet if either has hitherto
been only familiar with victory and triumph, never
yet having met with a foe that could cope with its
force, the first effect of a defeat, especially from
a despised adversary, unhinges and half paralyses
the whole nervous system. But as fighting Tom
gradually recovered to the consciousness of his
own strength, and the recollection that it had
been only foiled by the skilful trick of a wrestler,
not the hand-to-hand might of a pugilist, the panic
vanished, and Tom Bowles was himself again.

"Oh, that's your sort, is it?" said he. "We don't fight with our heels hereabouts, like Cornishers and donkeys; we fight with our fists, youngster; and since you *will* have a bout at that, why you must."

"Providence," answered Kenelm, solemnly, "sent me to this village for the express purpose of licking Tom Bowles. It is a signal mercy vouchsafed to yourself, as you will one day acknowledge."

Again a thrill of awe, something like that which the demagogue in Aristophanes might have felt when braved by the sausage-maker, shot through the valiant heart of Tom Bowles. He did not like those ominous words, and still less the lugubrious tone of voice in which they were uttered. But resolved, at least, to proceed to battle with more preparation than he had at first designed, he now deliberately disencumbered himself of his heavy fustian jacket and vest, rolled up his shirt-sleeves, and then slowly advanced towards the foe.

Kenelm had also, with still greater deliberation,

taken off his coat—which he folded up with care, as being both a new and an only one, and deposited by the hedge-side—and bared arms, lean indeed, and almost slight, as compared with the vast muscle of his adversary, but firm in sinew as the hind-leg of a stag.

By this time the labourers, led by Jessie, had arrived at the spot, and were about to crowd in between the combatants, when Kenelm waved them back, and said in a calm and impressive voice—

"Stand round, my good friends, make a ring, and see that it is fair play on my side. I am sure it will be fair on Mr. Bowles's. He's big enough to scorn what is little. And now, Mr. Bowles, just a word with you in the presence of your neighbours. I am not going to say anything uncivil. If you are rather rough and hasty, a man is not always master of himself—at least so I am told—when he thinks more than he ought to do about a pretty girl. But I can't look at your face even by this moonlight, and though its expression at this moment is rather cross, without being sure that you are a fine fellow at bottom. And that if you give a promise as man to man you will keep it. Is that so?"

One or two of the bystanders murmured assent; the others pressed round in silent wonder.

"What's all that soft-sawder about?" said Tom Bowles, somewhat falteringly.

"Simply this: if in the fight between us I beat you, I ask you to promise before your neighbours that you will not by word or deed molest or interfere again with Miss Jessie Wiles."

"Eh!" roared Tom. "Is it that *you* are after her?"

"Suppose I am, if that pleases you; and, on my side, I promise that, if you beat me, I quit this place as soon as you leave me well enough to do so, and will never visit it again. What! do you hesitate to promise? Are you really afraid I shall lick you?"

"You! I'd smash a dozen of you to powder."

"In that case, you are safe to promise. Come, 'tis a fair bargain. Isn't it, neighbours?"

Won over by Kenelm's easy show of good

temper, and by the sense of justice, the by-standers joined in a common exclamation of assent.

"Come, Tom," said an old fellow, "the gentle-man can't speak fairer; and we shall all think you be afeard if you hold back."

Tom's face worked; but at last he growled, "Well, I promise—that is, if he beats me."

"All right," said Kenelm. "You hear, neigh-bours; and Tom Bowles could not show that handsome face of his among you if he broke his word. Shake hands on it."

Fighting Tom sulkily shook hands.

"Well, now, that's what I call English," said Kenelm,—"all pluck and no malice. Fall back, friends, and leave a clear space for us."

The men all receded; and as Kenelm took his ground, there was a supple ease in his pos-ture which at once brought out into clearer evi-dence the nervous strength of his build, and, con-trasted with Tom's bulk of chest, made the latter look clumsy and top-heavy.

The two men faced each other a minute, the

eyes of both vigilant and steadfast. Tom's blood
began to fire up as he gazed—nor, with all his
outward calm, was Kenelm insensible of that
proud beat of the heart which is aroused by the
fierce joy of combat. Tom struck out first, and
a blow was parried, but not returned; another
and another blow—still parried—still unreturned.
Kenelm, acting evidently on the defensive, took
all the advantages for that strategy which he
derived from superior length of arm and lighter
agility of frame. Perhaps he wished to ascertain
the extent of his adversary's skill, or to try the
endurance of his wind, before he ventured on the
hazards of attack. Tom, galled to the quick that
blows which might have felled an ox were thus
warded off from their mark, and dimly aware that
he was encountering some mysterious skill which
turned his brute strength into waste force, and
might overmaster him in the long-run, came to a
rapid conclusion that the sooner he brought that
brute strength to bear, the better it would be for
him. Accordingly, after three rounds, in which,
without once breaking the guard of his antagonist,

he had received a few playful taps on the nose
and mouth, he drew back, and made a bull-like
rush at his foe—bull-like, for it butted full at him
with the powerful down-bent head, and the two
fists doing duty as horns. The rush spent, he
found himself in the position of a man *milled*. I
take it for granted that every Englishman who
can call himself a man—that is, every man who
has been an English boy, and, as such, been
compelled to the use of his fists—knows what a
'mill' is. But I sing not only "pueris," but "vir-
ginibus." Ladies,—'a mill'—using, with reluc-
tance and contempt for myself, that slang in
which lady-writers indulge, and Girls of the
Period know much better than they do their Mur-
ray—'a mill'—speaking not to lady-writers, not
to Girls of the Period, but to innocent damsels,
and in explanation to those foreigners who only
understand the English language as taught by
Addison and Macaulay—a 'mill,' periphrastically,
means this: your adversary, in the noble encounter
between fist and fist, has so plunged his head that
it gets caught, as in a vice, between the side and

doubled left arm of the adversary, exposing that head, unprotected and helpless, to be pounded out of recognisable shape by the right fist of the opponent. It is a situation in which raw superiority of force sometimes finds itself, and is seldom spared by disciplined superiority of skill. Kenelm, his right fist raised, paused for a moment, then, loosening the left arm, releasing the prisoner, and giving him a friendly slap on the shoulder, he turned round to the spectators, and said apologetically,—"He has a handsome face—it would be a shame to spoil it."

Tom's position of peril was so obvious to all, and that good-humoured abnegation of the advantage which the position gave to the adversary seemed so generous, that the labourers actually hurrahed. Tom himself felt as if treated like a child; and alas, and alas for him! in wheeling round, and regathering himself up, his eye rested on Jessie's face. Her lips were apart with breathless terror; he fancied they were apart with a smile of contempt. And now he became formidable. He fought as fights the bull in presence

of the heifer, who as he knows too well, will go
with the conqueror.

If Tom had never yet fought with a man
taught by a prize-fighter, so never yet had Kenelm
encountered a strength which, but for the lack of
that teaching, would have conquered his own.
He could act no longer on the defensive; he
could no longer play, like a dexterous fencer,
with the sledge-hammers of those mighty arms.
They broke through his guard—they sounded on
his chest as on an anvil. He felt that did they
alight on his head he was a lost man. He felt
also that the blows spent on the chest of his adversary were idle as the stroke of a cane on the
hide of a rhinoceros. But now his nostrils dilated,
his eyes flashed fire—Kenelm Chillingly had
ceased to be a philosopher. Crash came his blow
—how unlike the swinging roundabout hits of
Tom Bowles!—straight to its aim as the rifle-ball
of a Tyrolese, or a British marksman at Aldershot
—all the strength of nerve, sinew, purpose, and
mind concentred in its vigour,—crash just at that
part of the front where the eyes meet, and fol-

lowed up with the rapidity of lightning, flash upon flash, by a more restrained but more disabling blow with the left hand just where the left ear meets throat and jaw-bone.

At the first blow Tom Bowles had reeled and staggered, at the second he threw up his hands, made a jump in the air as if shot through the heart, and then heavily fell forwards, an inert mass.

The spectators pressed round him in terror. They thought he was dead. Kenelm knelt, passed quickly his hand over Tom's lips, pulse, and heart, and then rising, said, humbly and with an air of apology—

"If he had been a less magnificent creature, I assure you on my honour that I should never have ventured that second blow. The first would have done for any man less splendidly endowed by nature. Lift him gently; take him home. Tell his mother, with my kind regards, that I'll call and see her and him to-morrow. And, stop, does he ever drink too much beer?"

17*

"Well," said one of the villagers, "Tom *can* drink."

"I thought so. Too much flesh for that muscle. Go for the nearest doctor. You, my lad?—good —off with you—quick! No danger, but perhaps it may be a case for the lancet."

Tom Bowles was lifted tenderly by four of the stoutest men present and borne into his home, evincing no sign of consciousness; but his face, where not clouted with blood, very pale, very calm, with a slight froth at the lips.

Kenelm pulled down his shirt-sleeves, put on his coat, and turned to Jessie—

"Now, my young friend, show me Will's cottage."

The girl came to him white and trembling. She did not dare to speak. The stranger had become a new man in her eyes. Perhaps he frightened her as much as Tom Bowles had done. But she quickened her pace, leaving the public-house behind, till she came to the further end of the village. Kenelm walked beside her, muttering to himself; and though Jessie caught his words, happily she did not understand, for they repeated one of those bitter reproaches on her sex as the main cause of all strife, bloodshed, and mischief in general, with which the classic authors abound. His spleen soothed by that recourse to the lessons of the ancients, Kenelm turned at last to his silent companion, and said, kindly but gravely—

"Mr. Bowles has given me his promise, and it is fair that I should now ask a promise from you. It is this — just consider how easily a girl so pretty as you can be the cause of a man's death. Had Bowles struck me where I struck him, I should have been past the help of a surgeon."

"Oh!" groaned Jessie, shuddering, and covering her face with both hands.

"And, putting aside that danger, consider that a man may be hit mortally on the heart as well as on the head, and that a woman has much to answer for who, no matter what her excuse, forgets what misery and what guilt can be inflicted by a word from her lip and a glance from her eye. Consider this, and promise that, whether you marry Will Somers or not, you will never again give a man fair cause to think you can like him unless your own heart tells you that you can.   Will you promise that?"

"I will, indeed—indeed." Poor Jessie's voice died in sobs.

"There, my child, I don't ask you not to cry, because I know how much women like crying, and in this instance it does you a great deal of good.   But we are just at the end of the village: which is Will's cottage?"

Jessie lifted her head, and pointed to a solitary, small, thatched cottage.

"I would ask you to come in and introduce me; but that might look too much like crowing over poor Tom Bowles. So good-night to you, Jessie, and forgive me for preaching."

———

CHAPTER XIII.

KENELM knocked at the cottage door: a voice said faintly, "Come in."

He stooped his head, and stepped over the threshold.

Since his encounter with Tom Bowles his sympathies had gone with that unfortunate lover —it is natural to like a man after you have beaten him; and he was by no means predisposed to favour Jessie's preference for a sickly cripple.

Yet, when two bright, soft, dark eyes, and a pale intellectual countenance, with that nameless aspect of refinement which delicate health so often gives, especially to the young, greeted his quiet gaze, his heart was at once won over to the side of the rival. Will Somers was seated by the hearth, on which a few live embers, despite the warmth of the summer evening, still burned; a rude little table was by his side, on which were laid osier twigs and white peeled chips, together with an open

book. His hands, pale and slender, were at
work on a small basket half finished. His mother
was just clearing away the tea-things from another table that stood by the window. Will rose,
with the good breeding that belongs to the rural
peasant, as the stranger entered; the widow
looked round with surprise, and dropped her
simple courtesy—a little thin woman, with a mild
patient face.

The cottage was very tidily kept, as it is in
most village homes where the woman has it her
own way. The deal dresser opposite the door
had its display of humble crockery. The whitewashed walls were relieved with coloured prints,
chiefly Scriptural subjects from the New Testa-
ment, such as the return of the Prodigal Son, in
a blue coat and yellow inexpressibles, with his
stockings about his heels.

At one corner there were piled up baskets of
various sizes, and at another corner was an open
cupboard containing books—an article of de-
corative furniture found in cottages much more
rarely than coloured prints and gleaming crockery.

All this, of course, Kenelm could not at a glance comprehend in detail. But as the mind of a man accustomed to generalisation is marvellously quick in forming a sound judgment, whereas a mind accustomed to dwell only on detail is wonderfully slow at arriving at any judgment at all, and when it does, the probability is that it will arrive at a wrong one, Kenelm judged correctly when he came to this conclusion: "I am among simple English peasants; but, for some reason or other, not to be explained by the relative amount of wages, it is a favourable specimen of that class."

"I beg your pardon for intruding at this hour, Mrs. Somers," said Kenelm, who had been too familiar with peasants from his earliest childhood not to know how quickly, when in the presence of their household gods, they appreciate respect, and how acutely they feel the want of it. "But my stay in the village is very short, and I should not like to leave without seeing your son's basket-work, of which I have heard much."

"You are very good, sir," said Will, with a

pleased smile that wonderfully brightened up his
face. "It is only just a few common things that
I keep by me. Any finer sort of work I mostly
do by order."   •

"You see, sir," said Mrs. Somers, "it takes so
much more time for pretty work-baskets, and
suchlike; and unless done to order, it might be a
chance if he could get it sold. But pray be
seated, sir," and Mrs. Somers placed a chair for
her visitor, "while I just run upstairs for the
work-basket which my son has made for Miss
Travers. It is to go home to-morrow, and I put
it away for fear of accidents."

Kenelm seated himself, and, drawing his chair
near to Will's, took up the half-finished basket
which the young man had laid down on the
table.

"This seems to me very nice and delicate
workmanship," said Kenelm; "and the shape,
when you have finished it, will be elegant enough
to please the taste of a lady."

"It is for Mrs. Lethbridge," said Will; "she
wanted something to hold cards and letters;

and I took the shape from a book of drawings which Mr. Lethbridge kindly lent me. You know Mr. Lethbridge, sir? He is a very good gentleman."

"No, I don't know him. Who is he?"

"Our clergyman, sir. This is the book."

To Kenelm's surprise, it was a work on Pompeii, and contained woodcuts of the implements and ornaments, mosaics and frescoes, found in that memorable little city.

"I see this is your model," said Kenelm; "what they call a *patera*, and rather a famous one. You are copying it much more truthfully than I should have supposed it possible to do in substituting basket-work for bronze. But you observe that much of the beauty of this shallow bowl depends on the two doves perched on the brim. You can't manage that ornamental addition."

"Mrs. Lethbridge thought of putting there two little stuffed canary-birds."

"Did she? Good heavens!" exclaimed Kenelm.

"But somehow," continued Will, "I did not like that, and I made bold to say so."

"Why did not you like it?"

"Well, I don't know; but I did not think it would be the right thing."

"It would have been very bad taste, and spoilt the effect of your basket-work; and I'll endeavour to explain why. You see here, in the next page, a drawing of a very beautiful statue. Of course this statue is intended to be a representation of nature—but nature idealised. You don't know the meaning of that hard word, idealised, and very few people do. But it means the performance of a something in art according to the idea which a man's mind forms to itself out of a something in nature. That something in nature must, of course, have been carefully studied before the man can work out anything in art by which it is faithfully represented. The artist, for instance, who made that statue, must have known the proportions of the human frame. He must have made studies of various parts of it — heads and hands, and arms and legs, and so forth—and having done so, he then puts together all his various studies of details, so as to form a new whole, which is intended to personate an idea formed in his own mind. Do you go with me?"

"Partly, sir; but I'm puzzled a little still."

"Of course you are; but you'll puzzle yourself right if you think over what I say. Now if, in order to make this statue, which is composed of metal or stone, more natural, I stuck on it a wig of real hair, would not you feel at once that I had spoilt the work—that, as you clearly express it, 'it would not be the right thing?'—and, instead of·making the work of art more natural, I should have made it laughably unnatural, by forcing insensibly upon the mind of him who looked at it the contrast between the real life, represented by a wig of actual hair, and the artistic life, represented by an idea embodied in stone or metal. The higher the work of art (that is, the higher the idea it represents as a new combination of details taken from nature), the more it is degraded or spoilt by an attempt to give it a kind of reality which is out of keeping with the materials employed. But the same rule applies to everything in art, however humble,

And a couple of stuffed canary-birds at the brim of a basket-work imitation of a Greek drinking-cup, would be as bad taste as a wig from the barber's on the head of a marble statue of Apollo."

"I see," said Will, his head downcast, like a man pondering—"at least I think I see; and I'm very much obliged to you, sir."

Mrs. Somers had long since returned with the work-basket, but stood with it in her hands, not daring to interrupt the gentleman, and listening to his discourse with as much patience and as little comprehension as if it had been one of the controversial sermons upon Ritualism with which on great occasions Mr. Lethbridge favoured his congregation.

Kenelm having now exhausted his critical lecture—from which certain poets and novelists, who contrive to caricature the ideal by their attempt to put wigs of real hair upon the heads of stone statues, might borrow a useful hint or two if they would condescend to do so, which is not likely—perceived Mrs. Somers standing by him, took from her the basket, which was really very pretty and elegant, subdivided into various compartments for the implements in use among ladies, and bestowed on it a well-merited eulogium.

"The young lady means to finish it herself with ribbons, and line it with satin," said Mrs. Somers, proudly.

"The ribbons will not be amiss, sir?" said Will, interrogatively.

"Not at all. Your natural sense of the fitness of things tells you that ribbons go well with straw and light straw-like work such as this; though you would not put ribbons on those rude hampers and game-baskets in the corner. Like to like; a stout cord goes suitably with them; just as a poet who understands his art employs pretty expressions for poems intended to be pretty and suit a fashionable drawing-room, and carefully shuns them to substitute a simple cord for poems intended to be strong and travel far, despite of rough usage by the way. But you really ought to make much more money by this fancy-work than you could as a day-labourer."

Will sighed. "Not in this neighbourhood, sir. I might in a town."

"Why not move to a town, then?"

The young man coloured, and shook his head.

Kenelm turned appealingly to Mrs. Somers. "I'll be willing to go wherever it would be best for my boy, sir. But——". and here she checked herself, and a tear trickled silently down her cheeks.

Will resumed, in a more cheerful tone, "I am getting a little known now, and work will come if one waits for it."

Kenelm did not deem it courteous or discreet to intrude further on Will's confidence in the first interview; and he began to feel, more than he had done at first, not only the dull pain of the bruises he had received in the recent combat, but also somewhat more than the weariness which follows a long summer-day's work in the open air. He therefore, rather abruptly, now took his leave, saying that he should be very glad of a few specimens of Will's ingenuity and skill, and would call or write to give directions about them.

Just as he came in sight of Tom Bowles's

house on his way back to Mr. Saunderson's, Kenelm saw a man mounting a pony that stood tied up at the gate, and exchanging a few words with a respectable-looking woman before he rode on. He was passing by Kenelm without notice, when that philosophical vagrant stopped him, saying, "If I am not mistaken, sir, you are the doctor. There is not much the matter with Mr. Bowles?"

The doctor shook his head. "I can't say yet. He has had a very ugly blow somewhere."

"It was just under the left ear. I did not aim at that exact spot; but Bowles unluckily swerved a little aside at the moment, perhaps in surprise at a tap between his eyes immediately preceding it: and so, as you say, it was an ugly blow that he received. But if it cures him of the habit of giving ugly blows to other people who can bear them less safely, perhaps it may be all for his good, as, no doubt, sir, your schoolmaster said when he flogged you."

"Bless my soul! are you the man who fought with him—you? I can't believe it."

"Why not?"

"Why not! So far as I can judge by this light, though you are a tall fellow, Tom Bowles must be a much heavier weight than you are."

"Tom Spring was the champion of England; and according to the records of his weight, which History has preserved in her archives, Tom Spring was a lighter weight than I am?"

"But are you a prize-fighter?"

"I am as much that as I am anything else. But to return to Mr. Bowles, was it necessary to bleed him?"

"Yes; he was unconscious, or nearly so, when I came. I took away a few ounces, and I am happy to say he is now sensible, but must be kept very quiet."

"No doubt; but I hope he will be well enough to see me to-morrow."

"I hope so too; but I can't say yet. Quarrel about a girl—eh?"

"It was not about money. And I suppose if there were no money and no women in the world, there would be no quarrels, and very few doctors. Good night, sir."

"It is a strange thing to me," said Kenelm, as he now opened the garden-gate of Mr. Saunderson's homestead, "that though I've had nothing to eat all day, except a few pitiful sandwiches, I don't feel the least hungry. Such arrest of the lawful duties of the digestive organs never happened to me before. There must be something weird and ominous in it."

On entering the parlour, the family party, though they had long since finished supper, were still seated round the table. They all rose at sight of Kenelm. The fame of his achievements had preceded him. He checked the congratulations, the compliments, and the questions which the hearty farmer rapidly heaped upon him, with a melancholic exclamation, "But I have lost my appetite! No honours can compensate for that. Let me go to bed peaceably, and perhaps in the magic land of sleep Nature may restore me by a dream of supper."

CHAPTER XIV.

KENELM rose betimes the next morning somewhat stiff and uneasy, but sufficiently recovered
to feel ravenous. Fortunately one of the young
ladies who attended specially to the dairy was
already up, and supplied the starving hero with
a vast bowl of bread and milk. He then strolled
into the hay-field, in which there was now very
little left to do, and but few hands besides his
own were employed. Jessie was not there.
Kenelm was glad of that. By nine o'clock his
work was over, and the farmer and his men were
in the yard completing the ricks. Kenelm stole
away unobserved, bent on a round of visits. He
called first at the village shop kept by Mrs.
Bawtrey, which Jessie had pointed out to him,
on pretence of buying a gaudy neck-kerchief;
and soon, thanks to his habitual civility, made
familiar acquaintance with the shop-woman. She
was a little sickly old lady, her head shaking, as
with palsy, somewhat deaf, but still shrewd and
sharp, rendered mechanically so by long habits
of shrewdness and sharpness. She became very

communicative, spoke freely of her desire to give up the shop, and pass the rest of her days with a sister, widowed like herself, in a neighbouring town. Since she had lost her husband, the field and orchard attached to the shop had ceased to be profitable, and become a great care and trouble; and the attention the shop required was wearisome. But she had twelve years unexpired of the lease granted for twenty-one years to her husband on low terms, and she wanted a premium for its transfer, and a purchaser for the stock of the shop. Kenelm soon drew from her the amount of the sum she required for all—£45.

"You ben't thinking of it for yourself?" she asked, putting on her spectacles, and examining him with care.

"Perhaps so, if one could get a decent living out of it. Do you keep a book of your losses and gains?"

"In course, sir," she said, proudly. "I kept the books in my goodman's time, and he was one who could find out if there was a farthing wrong, for he had been in a lawyer's office when a lad."

"Why did he leave a lawyer's office to keep a little shop?"

"Well, he was born a farmer's son in this neighbourhood, and he always had a hankering after the country, and—and besides that——"

"Yes."

"I'll tell you the truth; he had got into a way of drinking speerrits, and he was a good young man, and wanted to break himself of it, and he took the temperance oath; but it was too hard on him, for he could not break himself of the company that led him into liquor. And so, one time when he came into the neighbourhood to see his parents for the Christmas holiday, he took a bit of liking to me; and my father, who was Squire Travers's bailiff, had just died, and left me a little money. And so, somehow or other, we came together, and got this house and the land from the Squire on lease very reasonable; and my goodman being well eddycated, and much thought of, and never being tempted to drink, now that he had a missus to keep him in order, had a many little things put into his way. He could help to measure timber, and knew about draining, and he got some book-keeping from the farmers about; and we kept cows and pigs and poultry, and so we did very well, specially as the Lord was merciful, and sent us no children."

"And what does the shop bring in a-year since your husband died?"

"You had best judge for yourself. Will you look at the book, and take a peep at the land and apple-trees? But they's been neglected since my goodman died."

In another minute the heir of the Chillinglys was seated in a neat little back parlour, with a pretty, though confined, view of the orchard and grass slope behind it, and bending over Mrs. Bawtrey's ledger.

Some customers for cheese and bacon coming now into the shop, the old woman left him to his studies. Though they were not of a nature familiar to him, he brought to them, at least, that general clearness of head and quick seizure of important points which are common to most men who have gone through some disciplined training of intellect, and been accustomed to extract the pith and marrow out of

many books on many subjects. The result of
his examination was satisfactory; there appeared
to him a clear balance of gain from the shop
alone of somewhat over £40 a-year, taking the
average of the last three years. Closing the
book, he then let himself out of the window into
the orchard, and thence into the neighbouring
grass field. Both were, indeed, much neglected;
the trees wanted pruning, the field manure. But
the soil was evidently of rich loam, and the fruit-
trees were abundant and of ripe age, generally
looking healthy in spite of neglect. With the
quick intuition of a man born and bred in the
country, and picking up scraps of rural knowledge unconsciously, Kenelm convinced himself
that the land, properly managed, would far more
than cover the rent, rates, tithes, and all in-
cidental outgoings, leaving the profits of the shop
as the clear income of the occupiers. And no
doubt, with clever young people to manage the
shop, its profits might be increased.

Not thinking it necessary to return at present
to Mrs. Bawtrey's, Kenelm now bent his way to
Tom Bowles's.

The house-door was closed. At the summons of his knock it was quickly opened by a tall, stout, remarkably fine-looking woman, who might have told fifty years, and carried them off lightly on her ample shoulders. She was dressed very respectably in black, her brown hair braided simply under a neat tight-fitting cap. Her features were aquiline and very regular— altogether, there was something about her majestic and Cornelia-like. She might have sat for the model of that Roman matron, except for the fairness of her Anglo-Saxon complexion.

"What's your pleasure?" she asked, in a cold and somewhat stern voice.

"Ma'am," answered Kenelm, uncovering, "I have called to see Mr. Bowles, and I sincerely hope he is well enough to let me do so."

"No, sir, he is not well enough for that; he is lying down in his own room, and must be kept quiet."

"May I then ask you the favour to let me in? I would say a few words to you who are his mother, if I mistake not."

Mrs. Bowles paused a moment as if in doubt;

but she was at no loss to detect in Kenelm's manner something superior to the fashion of his dress, and supposing the visit might refer to her son's professional business, she opened the door wider, drew aside to let him pass first, and when he stood midway in the parlour, requested him to take a seat, and to set him the example, seated herself.

"Ma'am," said Kenelm, "do not regret to have admitted me, and do not think hardly of me when I inform you that I am the unfortunate cause of your son's accident."

Mrs. Bowles rose with a start.

"You're the man who beat my boy?"

"No, ma'am, do not say I beat him. He is not beaten. He is so brave and so strong that he would easily have beaten me if I had not, by good luck, knocked him down before he had time to do so. Pray, ma'am, retain your seat and listen to me patiently for a few moments."

Mrs. Bowles, with an indignant heave of her Juno-like bosom, and with a superbly haughty expression of countenance, which suited well with its aquiline formation, tacitly obeyed.

"You will allow, ma'am," recommenced Kenelm, "that this is not the first time by many that Mr. Bowles has come to blows with another man. Am I not right in that assumption?"

"My son is of a hasty temper," replied Mrs. Bowles, reluctantly, "and people should not aggravate him."

"You grant the fact, then?" said Kenelm, imperturbably, but with a polite inclination of head. "Mr. Bowles has often been engaged in these encounters, and in all of them it is quite clear that he provoked the battle; for you must be aware that he is not the sort of man to whom any other would be disposed to give the first blow. Yet, after these little incidents had occurred, and Mr. Bowles had, say, half killed the person who aggravated him, you did not feel any resentment against that person, did you? Nay, if he had wanted nursing, you would have gone and nursed him."

"I don't know as to nursing," said Mrs. Bowles, beginning to lose her dignity of mien; "but certainly I should have been very sorry for him. And as for Tom—though I say it who should

not say—he has no more malice than a baby—
he'd go and make it up with any man, however
badly he had beaten him."

"Just as I supposed; and if the man had
sulked and would not make it up, Tom would
have called him a bad fellow, and felt inclined to
beat him again."

Mrs. Bowles's face relaxed into a stately smile.

"Well, then," pursued Kenelm, "I do but
humbly imitate Mr. Bowles, and I come to make
it up and shake hands with him."

"No, sir—no," exclaimed Mrs. Bowles, though
in a low voice, and turning pale. "Don't think
of it. 'Tis not the blows—he'll get over those
fast enough; 'tis his pride that's hurt; and if he
saw you there might be mischief. But you're a
stranger, and going away;—do go soon—do keep
out of his way—do!" And the mother clasped
her hands.

"Mrs. Bowles," said Kenelm, with a change of
voice and aspect—a voice and aspect so earnest
and impressive that they stilled and awed her—
"will you not help me to save your son from the
dangers into which that hasty temper and that

mischievous pride may at any moment hurry him. Does it never occur to you that these are the causes of terrible crime, bringing terrible punishment; and that against brute force, impelled by savage passions, society protects itself by the hulks and the gallows?"

"Sir, how dare you——"

"Hush! If one man kill another in a moment of ungovernable wrath, that is a crime which, though heavily punished by the conscience, is gently dealt with by the law, which calls it only manslaughter; but if a motive to the violence— such as jealousy or revenge—can be assigned, and there should be no witness by to prove that the violence was not premeditated, then the law does not call it manslaughter, but murder. Was it not that thought which made you so imploringly exclaim, 'Go soon; keep out of his way?'"

The woman made no answer, but sinking back in her chair, gasped for breath.

"Nay, madam," resumed Kenelm, mildly; "banish your fears. If you will help me I feel sure that I can save your son from such perils, and I only ask you to let me save him. I am convinced that he has a good and a noble nature, and he is worth saving." As he thus said he took her hand. She resigned it to him and returned the pressure, all her pride softening as she began to weep.

At length, when she recovered voice, she said—

"It is all along of that girl. He was not so till she crossed him, and made him half mad. He is not the same man since then—my poor Tom!"

"Do you know that he has given me his word, and before his fellow-villagers, that if he had the worst of the fight he would never molest Jessie Wiles again?"

"Yes, he told me so himself; and it is that which weighs on him now. He broods, and broods, and mutters, and will not be comforted; and—and I do fear that he means revenge. And, again, I implore you keep out of his way."

"It is not revenge on me that he thinks of. Suppose I go and am seen no more, do you think in your own heart that that girl's life is safe?"

"What! My Tom kill a woman!"

"Do you never read in your newspaper of a

man who kills his sweetheart, or the girl who re-
fuses to be his sweetheart? At all events, you
yourself do not approve this frantic suit of his.
If I have heard rightly, you have wished to get
Tom out of the village for some time, till Jessie
Wiles is—we'll say, married, or gone elsewhere
for good."

"Yes, indeed, I have wished and prayed for it
many's the time, both for her sake and for his.
And I am sure I don't know what we shall do if
he stays, for he has been losing custom fast. The
Squire has taken away his, and so have many of
the farmers; and such a trade as it was in his
good father's time! And if he would go, his
uncle, the Veterinary at Luscombe, would take
him into partnership; for he has no son of his
own, and he knows how clever Tom is;—there
ben't a man who knows more about horses; and
cows, too, for the matter of that."

"And if Luscombe is a large place, the business there must be more profitable than it can be
here, even if Tom got back his custom?"

"Oh yes! five times as good—if he would but
go; but he'll not hear of it."

"Mrs. Bowles, I am **very** much obliged to you for your confidence, **and I feel** sure that all will end happily, **now we have had this talk.** I'll not press farther **on** you at **present.** Tom will not stir out, I suppose, till **the evening.**"

"Ah, sir, he seems **as if he** had no heart to stir out again, unless for something dreadful."

"Courage! I will call again in the evening, and then you just take me up to Tom's room, and leave me there to make friends with him, as I have with you. Don't say a word about me in the meanwhile."

"But——"

"'But,' Mrs. Bowles, is a word that cools many a warm impulse, stifles many a kindly thought, puts a dead stop to many a brotherly deed. Nobody would ever love his neighbour as himself if he listened to all the Buts that could be said on the other side of the question."

END OF VOL. I.

PRINTING OFFICE OF THE PUBLISHER.

www.ingramcontent.com/pod-product-compliance
Lightning Source LLC
Chambersburg PA
CBHW020511270326
41926CB00008B/831